Reckless Faith

LET GO AND BE LED

Reckless Faith

LET GO AND BE LED

BETH GUCKENBERGER

ZONDERVAN®

ZONDERVAN.com/
AUTHORTRACKER
follow your favorite authors

Reckless Faith
Copyright © 2008 by Beth Guckenberger

Requests for information should be addressed to:
Zondervan, *Grand Rapids, Michigan* 49530

Library of Congress Cataloging-in-Publication Data

Guckenberger, Beth, 1972 –
    Reckless faith / Beth Guckenberger.
       p. cm.
    ISBN 978-0-310-28393-5 (softcover : alk. paper)
    1. Guckenberger, Beth, 1972 – 2. Missionaries — Biography. 3. Church work with
orphans. 4. Church work with children. 5. Trust in God. I. Title.
    BV2622.G83A3 2008
    266.0092 — dc220

                         2008007381

Interior design by Christine Orejuela-Winkelman

Printed in the United States of America

08 09 10 11 12 • 22 21 20 19 18 17 16 15 14 13 12 11 10 9 8 7 6 5 4 3 2 1

To my parents,
Allen and Ruth Ewing,
before I knew what God thought of me,
I knew what you thought of me,
and it set me up to follow
your reckless faith ...

Contents

God loves it when the giver delights in the giving. God can pour on the blessings in astonishing ways so that you're ready for anything and everything, more than just ready to do what needs to be done. As one psalmist puts it, "He throws caution to the winds, giving to the needy in reckless abandon."

2 Corinthians 9:7 – 9 MSG

Introduction

I'm a long way from Sunday Lane.

That thought flitters through my mind, and I stifle a laugh. There's nothing funny about where I am now, but laughing makes me less fearful. On Sunday Lane in Maineville, Ohio, I learned how to climb trees, how to talk to Jewish children, how to make chocolate chip cookies, and how to drive. Riding down that street on our tandem bicycle, I had a hunch not everyone lived like we did — but I could never have imagined a street like the one I now find myself on.

Imagine standing on a multilane roadway in Tirana, Albania, with every vehicle imaginable rushing by us as fast as it knows how. What causes me to notice the little boy, I don't know, but there he is, seemingly lifeless, lying face-down on the cobblestones.

As I reach down to pick him up, I see that he's just a toddler, but before I can lift him, a soldier points a machine gun at me and orders me to back up. I do.

My fiancé, Todd, says, "Beth, ... just listen to him. I'm going to get the translator." He starts walking backward, never breaking our gaze.

It's 1994, and we are serving with Campus Crusade for Christ for two weeks over our spring break from college. I haven't even learned how to ask for water in Albanian, so negotiating with this officer about an abandoned child seems impossible. I know the key phrases for the "Four

The little boy we stopped to pick up in Albania

Spiritual Laws," but he doesn't look like a receptive audience.

The officer seems as relieved as I am when the translator arrives. "The boy is property of the gypsies," the translator explains what the officer is saying. "They keep him awake all night so he'll sleep in the streets all day. People walk by and throw money at him, which the gypsies collect when they come to get him at dusk."

Why do the authorities let them do this? I wonder. Does this officer know the boy's caretaker? Why won't he let me touch him? Perhaps he shares in the spoils.

"It's too dangerous for him just to be left here," I say. Then I ask, "What stops me — or anybody — from just picking him up right now and walking away with him?" I stand there, waiting for an answer.

Listen carefully: Unless a grain of wheat is buried in the ground, dead to the world, it is never any more than a grain of wheat. But if it is buried, it sprouts and reproduces itself many times over. In the same way, anyone who holds on to life just as it is, destroys that life. But if you let it go, reckless in your love, you'll have it forever, real and eternal. If any of you wants to serve me, then follow me. Then you'll be where I am, ready to serve at a moment's notice. The Father will honor and reward anyone who serves me.

John 12:24–26 MSG

Learn to do good; Seek justice, Reprove the ruthless, Defend the orphan, Plead for the widow.

Isaiah 1:17 NASB

Those passages move me. The rest of the book you have in your hands is the story of how these truths have played out in my life. For a long time, I hesitated even writing this book, wondering whether I could really make it worthy of a subject that's so important to me — the subject of reckless faith. While I long to love and give recklessly, I admit that there are days when I don't.

But the idea of living a reckless faith still captivates me.

As a child I used to sing songs about the Refiner's fire. The analogy is of silver and dross. As the fire heats the silver, the impurities come to the surface and are skimmed off, leaving the silver more and more refined. In the analogy, *refined* means "pure," and naturally I want the impurities of sin to come to the surface, so that my faith can be ever more pure. That kind of refinement is part of what the Holy Spirit draws us to with each conviction and subsequent confession.

But *refined* can also be defined as "cultivated" and "fastidious." That kind of "refined faith" is the opposite of the reckless faith I'm writing about here. That sort of "refined faith" is predictable and resistant to change; it pretends to know what God will do a hundred Sundays from now. It is most comfortable with rules, consequences, and baby steps. It likes control and people who agree. It fears what it can't see. A truly reckless faith, however, always expects change, and as a result, it's eager to risk *more* and fear *less*! A reckless faith knows there is more to the story, more we can't see, more than I experience now. It is hungry.

While watching the movie *It's a Wonderful Life* the other night with my family, I saw a sign on the wall of George Bailey's office. (Jimmy Stewart plays George, a kind man who places people before profit in a savings and loan business.) The sign reads, "You can only take with you what you have given away." George was on to something there. A reckless faith is more concerned with the balance of what you've given than what you have left.

On the flight back from Albania, we talk about the little boy.

Reckless faith always has one foot in eternity. It measures people by their actions and not their belongings. A reckless faith believes when there is no evidence and hurls itself at what is unseen but promised. A reckless faith isn't "refined" in the least. It does not make sense to the world, and yet, the world often seems fascinated by it.

The Albanian officer just keeps looking at me as I eye his machine gun. Through the translator, he finally answers my question: "Well, first, if you took the child away, you'd be taking him away from his legal caretaker; she'd probably just place another child here. Nothing would change. And second, it's the only life he's ever known. What else would he do?" He shrugs and turns around, dismissing me. He has bigger concerns than the boy and this curious tourist.

Todd and I sit on a park bench nearby and watch the boy sleep for the better part of an hour. That question, "What else would he do?" keeps rolling around in my mind. I pray for the child and his mother, and I pray for my questions and the anger I feel. I pray for his country and the other children like him, certain to be lying on their own street corners.

And then I pray that I might have a hand in helping rescue a life like his.

Todd and I take a picture of him and begin to talk about what we can do. It's as though the wind is blowing, and we aren't sure from where it's coming, but we can see the leaves kicking up.

The next day, we visit our first orphanage, filled with children like our boy on the street. We're only there for an hour or so — almost as an afterthought. We just happened to be walking by and saw kids hanging out of the windows. So we thought we'd stop in and visit. I sit on a concrete step on the second floor with a child on each knee, and I feel as though the wind has stopped.

I feel as though I'm home.

The stories in the chapters that follow aren't chronological. They're not a history of how I found myself living on the side of a mountain in Mexico, and I'm not sure that would interest anyone but my mother and her friends anyway. Instead, I've mined my journals for those moments when God used the very people I thought I was in Mexico to lead, to lead me. Time and again I've been led to trust God, with my little mustard seed of faith, to see how he not only shows up in our circumstance — but he shows off! It's not because he needs to prove himself; rather, he is demonstrating to a forgotten population — the orphans that I serve — that he will be their Father and Protector and Provider.

> *You are the light of the world. A city set on a hill cannot be hidden; nor does anyone light a lamp and put it under a basket, but on the lampstand, and it gives light to all who are in the house.*
>
> *Let your light shine before men in such a way that they may see your good works, and glorify your Father who is in heaven.*
>
> Matthew 5:14 – 16 NASB
>
> *In the same way, anyone who holds on to life just as it is, destroys that life. But if you let it go, reckless in your love, you'll have it forever, real and eternal.*
>
> John 12:25 MSG

Before reading this book, however, ponder some statistics:

- 143.5 million children worldwide have lost one or both parents.
- The proportion of children who are orphans generally increases with age.
- 12% (17.5 million) are 0 – 5 years old.
- 33% (47 million) are 6 – 11 years old.
- 55% (79 million) are 12 – 17 years old.

ONE

The Little Girl

It's almost the end of the week, and we've run out of projects, supplies, and motivation.

For the past few years Todd and I have sponsored our church's youth mission trips to Queretaro, Mexico. In general, we know what to expect. A little paint here, a little polish there, some late-night tacos, an evangelistic drama — all in the name of the Lord.

The truth is, no one really cares. As I unpack the paints, I think, "Haven't we painted this wall before?" We are frustrated, the students are uninspired, and worst of all, the nationals we have come to serve are unaffected.

One of the men from our group comes up to us and says, "About two more hours, and we can clean up here and head for dinner."

"Two hours, huh?" I sigh.

I close my eyes and try to think how to fill that time, until Todd interrupts my thoughts: "Remember the orphanage we visited in Albania?" he asks, his back to me, bent over, cleaning some paintbrushes.

"Sure. Why?"

"You think there are any in this town?"

Even before he can stand up and turn around, I'm gone. I dash over to where our teens are talking to some of their Mexican counterparts.

"*Orphanage-o*? *Orphanatorio*? *Orphanagorio*?" I try every combination with my best Mexican accent to get a reaction. "*Aquí*?" ("Here?")

"*Sí. Sí.*" They look at me laughing, either because the answer is obvious or because of my funny words. I don't know which.

I wish I could say that Todd and I sat down right then and made a plan, but we didn't. The truth is, within ten minutes of his question, we leave the students with the other adult sponsors, and we're in a taxi trying to find an orphanage.

Looking back now, it seems foolish. We didn't speak much Spanish, didn't have much money if we got into trouble, and were in a city where we could have easily gotten lost. An hour later, we're standing in front of a children's home on a dusty road, knocking at the door as we wave goodbye to our taxi driver.

We hear a series of locks, bolts, and chains being unlatched, and the door swings open. Have you ever heard the expression "his face is an open book"? Well, the title of the book on the face of the man who answers the door is *Who the Heck Are You?* Even though he's sitting in a wheelchair, he seems eight feet tall. Seeing him makes us wonder if all those locks are to keep people out or keep children in. While he waits for us to explain ourselves, I catch a glimpse of a child over his shoulder.

Todd stumbles through some high school Spanish phrases, and, perhaps out of pity, the man lets us in. As we round the corner, more children come into view, and though they stare at us questioningly, I'm instantly captivated. To them, we must look a sight — still in our paint clothes and probably looking stranger than anyone they've ever seen.

We struggle with our bad Spanish for more than an hour but don't get far. Finally, frustrated, Todd gives up and starts playing basketball with some of the boys, leaving me to continue the conversation with Mr. Congeniality. For a while we watch Todd in silence, our host with a blank expression on his face and me hoping we really are on a holy errand.

The thought crosses my mind, has this man already asked us to leave in Spanish and we just didn't understand? Or is this something that you planned, Lord?

Finally, the man turns to me and says, "I can understand you. I'm an American."

I can't believe it. Why did he pretend? I know I should be mad — but my first thought is gratitude that we can now communicate.

He continues, "I'm a Vietnam War vet. I came to work with abandoned children because I know what it means to be tossed aside. Like them, I'm trying to forget the people who failed me. I don't always trust outsiders."

I say nothing.

Todd, who has overheard everything, walks over from the court, with the ball under his arm, and says, "We have two hundred dollars, twenty-five eager students, and a whole day left in our trip. Is there anything we can do for you if we come back tomorrow?"

The man shifts his eyes and says softly, "The children haven't had meat in a year, and that window up there is broken."

Sometimes just talking can cost you. His admission costs him something, and our request costs us as well. We all overcome our fears and say things that are uncomfortable. But we do it. As we sit there on that bench, sipping our lemonade, I know what's happened: our first *real* mission has begun.

The next day, with a much clearer sense of purpose, we set out for the children's home. On the way, we stop at a market to buy food and toys. When we get to the front door, the children are waiting, laughing, and asking if "Michael Jordan" has come back.

We have two hundred hamburgers, a new window, and our crew of teenagers.

The orphanage is built like a bullfighting arena, with a large open area in the middle. Steep stairs go up to the

This is me with my friend Elisa, who is the same age as the little girl I followed.

dorms on the top layer, which encircle the courtyard below. We set up the grill in the courtyard and begin serving the meal.

After all forty of the kids receive their hamburgers and second helpings, we find ourselves still flipping burgers. From behind the grill, Todd whispers, "What's going on? These kids can't still be hungry; go see if you can figure out where all the food's wandering off to."

So I mingle with the kids, who are holding napkins full of hamburgers. Some are carrying them up to their rooms; and I follow one little preschool girl up the stairs to the dormitory, and with each step, it's almost as if I can feel her leading me, wanting me to see something. When we reach the top, she hesitates only slightly as she enters and leaves me standing in the doorway.

She's hiding the hamburger patties under her mattress.

When I walk into the room, some of the other girls are startled and one of them starts to cry. Why? Do they think I'll be mad? Yell at them? Hit them? Take the hamburgers back? I don't know, but none of those things even occur to me. I simply help the little girl I followed lift her heavy mattress.

After we carefully hide the girl's hamburger, I take her hand, and we head back out the door. Then I stop and send her down to get Todd. After he bounds up the stairs, we stand together in that doorway, and something happens to us, right there, that we don't even realize at the time. But when I chart the events of my life that followed, they trace back to that moment in the doorway.

We walk slowly down the stairs, trying to think of how we might be able to buy more hamburgers. At the bottom, the director is watching us skeptically, waiting for our reaction, and he explains that the kids often save food for later. Even though we know the hamburgers won't keep long, none of us has the heart to stop them.

That day Todd and I had a *defining moment* — an experience that impacted our thinking, touched our hearts, and compelled us into a new course of action. It changed our lives. I used to be afraid of that word, *change*, as if it implied, somehow, that I need to be corrected. But now I have a different view of change. It is a shift in perspective and not the Extreme Home Makeover kind of change we see on television. It is a shift

> in what we think we are capable of.
> in where we want to see our life heading.
> in how we are willing to spend our time, talents, and resources.

When people tell me about how God "moved" them, it is that kind of shift, I believe, they are talking about. It's a step in a new direction that we couldn't have taken on our own. Sometimes defining moments result in immediate and complete life transformations, like it did for the apostle Paul on the road to Damascus; but more often, such moments are more subtle, things we can only see in hindsight.

For me, the hamburger incident was not a defining moment that lit up in neon lights. Not at all. I flew home the next day, went back to work, headed to the grocery store, called my friends — but there was a difference. I have since described it as being like a burr under my saddle. I knew I would never feel quite comfortable again. Something inside me *had* shifted, and after the supernatural pleasure of that "defining moment," like an addict, I knew I wanted another hit.

Before that trip to Mexico, I was not a bad person. I wasn't doing anything wrong that required major discipline in my life. But that trip was more like a big wooden marker in the shape of an arrow pointing to someplace I couldn't see — a place I was nervous about, but excited to explore. Just a week before the trip, the path I was on in my life had seemed fine, but now, in light of that experience, I didn't want fine anymore. For a year afterward, I moved around on that saddle trying to get comfortable again, but there was that silly burr, always reminding me that I had changed that afternoon in Mexico. That is what reckless faith does — it propels me faster and harder towards God's true plan for my life.

Todd and I talked hundreds of hours in the following year about those hamburgers and about all the people we knew who could buy food for orphans if they only knew there was a need and how important they could be in meeting that need. It became clear that the arrow was pointing us back

to Mexico, and so, without much guidance other than a vague sense of the rightness of the decision, we moved to Monterrey.

Today, when people look at our organization and ask about strategy, vision casting, projection, and planning, we just smile. It would be tempting to spin it all so it seems more polished.

But the truth is, it started with a little girl hiding a hamburger under her mattress.

Two

Change of Plan

What seemed romantic at first is now just hot.

In the first few days after arriving in Mexico to live, we struggle to get our utilities hooked up, wander aimlessly for half a day in Wal-Mart just because it's air-conditioned, get lost more times than we are found, order shaved turkey that turns out to be pastrami, and kill cockroaches the size of my fist. But we also meet our first orphan, and we're reminded why we're here.

In the months leading up to our move, we bought a map of Mexico and studied it. Which city do we move to? Do we throw a dart? I was voting for the ones near the ocean but was outvoted by Todd, who chose Monterrey because we knew a family from Cincinnati who was moving back there after a stint in our university town. Luis and Alma Alvarado were our 911 call, our only friends in Mexico and our substitute family that first year. They were the ones who directed us down the highway to our first orphanage.

At the orphanage, we scramble out of the car. Todd goes looking for the office, or at least an adult, and I make a bee-line toward the first child I see.

"*Hola!*" I say, practically overwhelming her to the point of tears.

"*Hola*," she responds shyly.

I reach out for her hand, but she moves it away. I know how to recite our address, order from McDonald's, and make a clear presentation of the gospel — all in Spanish — but none of that seems appropriate at the moment. So I just smile back. We're both a little relieved when Todd calls me away, though I wonder what he can possibly need from me more than this little girl does.

Todd and I walk together into what looks like an office and try to explain to a couple of the staff mingling in the office that we are there to help, that for the next year we want "to be able to meet their most deeply felt needs." The only *problemo* is that they don't understand us. Not our words, nor our intentions. The mingling stops. The staring starts.

But after our experience in Quaretaro the year before, we've become quick learners. Wasting no time, I pick up a baby, and Todd grabs a broom.

The little girl I talked to before sidles up to me, points to the baby, and says, "Lupita."

"Loopy-ta?" I try to make my tongue sound like hers.

She dissolves into giggles and I join her.

I look up and catch Todd's eye across the room. He is knocking on the wall, listening for beams or termites or soundness, or something. He smiles at me from a deep place, and I smile back. We're home.

Semana Santa, the week before Easter, is the busiest week of the year in Mexico. Since the crucified Christ is the preeminent symbol of faith to this Catholic nation, the celebrations of that week are even more important than Christmas. The whole country goes on spring break, adults and children alike, and there is a party on every street corner.

Todd and I have agreed to host eighty people from Oklahoma at our mission that week. Since we can't ignore what is happening in the city, and just going about our normal business would make no sense, we decided to engage our visitors with the culture and do an outreach in a busy suburb of the city.

We also want the children of the orphanage to participate in an outreach experience, so we round up our eighty visitors from Oklahoma along with several dozen children. Arriving in the suburb, we stream out of the buses that hot Saturday afternoon carrying two thousand cold Cokes and invitations to a passion play that our Mexican church is presenting at a local theater later that evening.

That is our plan, and I am convinced that this is God's design for the day. I plan not to stray from it.

As we break into teams, I sit in a central location and, with my clipboard and my visor and my unchangeable goal, I supervise.

But about halfway through the afternoon, I'm called over to solve a problem. On my way, I bump into a woman and mutter, "*Con permiso*," and not to be deterred, I keep on going. I'm there to pass out invitations. This is the big deal — an impressive plan.

Meanwhile, one of the young men from Oklahoma, who is trailing along in the wake of my determination, tries to strike up a conversation with the woman I brushed by. After exhausting his Spanish, he comes to get my attention.

"That lady over there ... I *think* she said she either has an orphanage or is one or has visited one or wants one ... I don't know ... something along those lines. I think you should talk to her."

I look at him and then close my eyes in response to the hair now standing up on my neck — which is a big deal considering the amount of sweat that's there. Before I even turn around, I can feel the Holy Spirit leap inside me.

Pay attention, Ewing. I know it's serious when that voice inside me uses my maiden name. I sigh, adjust my visor, glance at my clipboard, and hand it off to someone else.

When I turn around, more than two dozen little children, all dressed alike, are standing behind this woman, staring at me. I bet they're wondering what's so important that I needed to buzz completely past them.

That afternoon I meet Mama Cony and the children who live with her. For more than two decades she and her husband, Chuy, have provided shelter to children who have nowhere else to go. On the day I meet her, almost forty of them live in Mama Cony and Chuy's little house. God in heaven knows that she and her husband have some tremendous responsibilities and needs, and they have cried out to him and trust him to bring help. On that day, once she had put matters into God's hands and stopped wringing her own, she took her children on a walk on a beautiful afternoon during *Semana Santa*.

Today, Mama Cony's ministry serves more than four times as many children as she did on the day we met. She now has three homes instead of one and probably has plans for three more. God was writing a story in heaven for Samuel and Lydia and Gaby and José, and his grand plan to protect them involved a chance meeting on a hot afternoon in Mexico during *Semana Santa*.

That young man from Oklahoma set off a chain of events that led to our fulfilling a God-ordained destiny. Boy, am I ever glad he chose today to try out his Spanish!

We had a divine appointment that afternoon — but I had almost missed the Plan behind the plan because I was so busy with my agenda. It's not that the two thousand Cokes weren't used by God. I am sure that they were. Someday in heaven I will find out which of those recipients of a Coke and an invitation to the play came forward to profess faith in Christ afterward, but I have a hunch that God was also prompting a teenager from Oklahoma to be more bold about his faith. And God had a lesson or two for me as well. And one for Mama Cony to boot.

Isn't it hard to let go of our plans? Sometimes I'm so sure of myself, so confident that whatever is hardest to pull off, whatever is splashier or pays the biggest returns, is always God's plan. Sometimes I think he looks at the little boy with the loaves instead of the grown man with the fancy plans. He looks at the woman with the perfume bottle rather than the spiritual leader hosting the lunch. He looks at the boy with the sling rather than the army.

We live in the only desert, as far as I know, to be hit by a hurricane.

Most days it's so hot and dry that my neighbors pour water on the dirt road to cut down on the dust in their homes. Monterrey is hours away from the nearest ocean. But since we are situated deep inside a mountain ravine, some combination of air currents and wind and weather made us ripe for Hurricane Emily, which blew over from the Gulf of Mexico. If it hadn't been so horrible, the irony would have been comical.

On the day of the hurricane, as a light rain begins to fall, we gather under a thatched roof *palapa* to plan our response to the coming storm. A team of people from Ohio is visiting that week, and although they came to serve orphans, we are now talking about how we can serve all the poor who are soon to suffer. I was nervous that the team wouldn't make that jump with us, but they show up under the *palapa* that morning with garbage-bag raincoats and a sense of willingness.

"What can we do?" says Mark, their trip leader.

"We need to start with the orphanages," says Todd, "then we'll move out into the squatter villages. First we need to help tarp the shacks to minimize wind and rain damage. Then we'll help stock up food and water supplies, so that if people are trapped for days, they'll survive."

Everyone sits silent. *Trapped for days*? Interrupting everybody's thoughts, Mark says, "Whatever you need, we'll help. We're here for you to use us as God leads."

That afternoon we plan, shop for supplies, and make emergency food kits. The next morning, the team travels to an area we call "the Rio," located on a riverbank. It's normally pleasant as far as squatter villages go, since it is cooler and provides water for bathing and washing clothes, but in this case, the location presents more danger than protection.

When we arrive, there's already lots of activity. The government is traveling around volunteering to shuttle people in low-income areas to government buildings, like schools and firehouses.

"*Vamos, te ayudo.*" We teach our team this key phrase, "Let's go; I'll help you," to use as they help people leave the area and board the buses. Some of the locals willingly leave with the first shift, and with our encouragement another round packs up their things and goes on the next run. But by the end of the day, there are still about fifteen people who refuse to leave what looks stable for a threat that is still only perceived.

"Mark," Todd starts in, looking around, "I think we need to stay here a little longer and build a bridge over that creek in case the waters do indeed come and these fifteen people stubbornly stay put. I don't know how else they'll get out."

This is the area where the rains came and the bridge was built.

The guys survey the scene and see the team already starting to lean against the bus, finishing up their water bottles, and giving each other backrubs. It has been a long day. A few are cleaning up or engaging with the children who are milling around.

"Okay," Mark says. "If there's work to be done, let's get started."

They call over the whole team and pray for energy, materials, light, and for the rains to hold off. They then begin construction of a simple wooden platform over a ravine that is starting to fill with the early rains.

After they finish, they gather the remaining workers together and pray again over the bridge: "Lord, you led us here and to this work. Please use it to accomplish what is your will in the lives of these new friends ..." Then the group leaves for their own safety.

For days, the phones are out of order and the streets flooded. We see from television footage how the waters have overcome some communities and we are heartsick, wondering if the families we cared for got to safety. We make hot food and pass it out to homes where they usually cook over wood that is now wet, and we wait.

Then the call comes. It is breathless, tearful, and glorious.

"Halleujah! I have news to report!" Our contact was calling from a pay phone.

"*Las lluvias* weren't stopping, and the families weren't moving out, and the severity of the situation had set in. Everyone was starting to feel worried; then they became paralyzed with fear. From the bank up ahead the authorities bullhorned down to the ravine, and ordered all of us to evacuate."

"But you are calling me, right? So you are out and safe?!" I was trying to jump to the end of the story.

She continues, "There was nowhere to cross the river except for the bridge. When the police called down, the families didn't hesitate and scrambled over it to safety. That little bridge saved our lives!"

A moment more of hallelujahs and then we promised to connect when the roads were clear. I hung up the phone and thought about the outcome if our friends from Northstar

Vineyard had shook their heads and said, "We came here to work with orphans. We are not here to build bridges or stomp around a muddy river in the rain!" What opportunities would have been missed?

These days I try to be on the lookout constantly and to be present enough in the moment to catch an opportunity to let the light inside me shine. To do that, I sometimes need to bite my tongue when I want to share my opinion, and I sometimes turn my watch around on my wrist so I won't be distracted by it. I try to look into the coming storm and ask, "How can I help?" instead of thinking about what plans are being disrupted or what inconveniences I might experience.

Not all opportunities become defining moments, nor do they always result in the saving of lives, but I realize, more and more, that our paths are littered with burrs in saddles, hamburgers under mattresses, women we "bump" into, and storms from which we can offer shelter. God's plan is for more than just my eternal salvation. He has a plan for my entire earthly life. Once I have him as a guide, will the journeys all end at the same stop? Yes, I think so. With him as my Savior, I know a heavenly home is being built for me that I will one day enjoy for eternity.

One path through life looks about as exciting as the desert I drive through to reach Texas — flat, plain, the scenery all the same. But there's another journey through life that is technicolored, filled with moments when I say, "I am open to the person, relationship, experience, task, or risk you might have for me here."

Each person, relationship, experience, task, or risk changes not just what I can see, but more importantly, changes *me*.

I am not more reckless because I helped poor people tarp up their shacks or held an orphan baby. I am more reckless because when I felt uncomfortable in that orphanage, I didn't run away, and when I got tired of being wet, I stayed to help. Reckless faith isn't determined by my circumstances; I don't have hurricanes and Coke giveaways every day. It is born and can grow daily in the quiet moments when my flesh and spirit collide and I decide to let it happen.

THREE

Joel

Pleas for more food are ringing in Edgar's ears.

He's the director of a children's home with over fifty children, and he carries the burden of providing for each one. It is November and starting to get cold. "Should we use our remaining money for heat, blankets, or food?" he wonders.

Had Edgar picked up the phone and called our ministry, we would have brought over some food for the evening meal. But in his heart Edgar knew that neither he nor the children should grow dependent on mere humans. It wasn't pride that kept him from calling us that afternoon; rather it was a fear that the children would be tempted to put humans on the pedestal that is fit only for a King.

So Edgar prays. Then he decides to have the children join him in his prayers. That Saturday afternoon, he and the children sit down to pray for a dinner they have not yet received: "Dear Lord, we thank you for your numerous blessings on these children and for this home. We humbly ask that you would provide a meal for us tonight — "

Children praying for their meal at one of the homes

Suddenly he is interrupted by Joel, one of the youngest boys. "*Tío*," says Joel slowly, "we're praying for God to bring us dinner? What kind of food *does* God deliver?"

Edgar, always looking for a teachable moment, wants to instill in the children that it is God who provides all blessings, so he seizes this chance. "Joel, God loves you and you are his child. He wants you to know he sees you and wants to lavish his riches on you. Let's just see what he will deliver."

They begin to pray again.

Soon Joel interrupts him again to ask, "Do you think ... Will the Lord bring us ... meat?"

To a little boy whose diet is mainly beans and rice, tortillas and hot dogs, meat seems like a mighty request. Edgar challenges him to ask anything in the Lord's name and expect him to respond.

So they bow their heads again, praying for dinner and meat in Jesus' name, until Joel can't stand it any longer. He asks (in the way preschoolers love to continue on with their questioning), "*Tío*, what *kind* of meat does God bring?"

That same day, a man named Carlos flies into Monterrey on business at the convention center and calls us late in the afternoon. Do we remember meeting him earlier in the year in Cincinnati? Are we interested in joining him for dinner?

I remember meeting him and talking about how he occasionally travels to Monterrey, but I have lost his card.

We arrange to meet at 6:00 p.m., but he quickly calls back to ask if we can bring a pick up truck. It seems there is a lot of extra "product" he has flown in for the vendor sale, and it had been thawing all day and is no longer of use to him.

After confessing that I have forgotten his line of business, he politely answers that he represents a meat company and has flown in all kinds of meat for potential vendors at a food fair, some of the best cuts available. All his orders have been placed, and now he is just going to discard the samples, which had been thawing all day. So, he wants to know, can we use a donation of high-end cuts of meat?

That evening, as Todd drives home from the convention center, with the bed of his truck overflowing with some of the best meats money can buy, he calls me. "Beth, this is way more than our freezer can handle. I'm going to start dropping it off at the orphanages on the way home. Will you call and let them know I'm coming?"

Joel's home is the first one on his route.

When I call the children's home, Edgar doesn't seem surprised. He asks me calmly, "Do you know what kind of food it is?"

"Some kind of meat, Edgar," I answer. "I'm not totally sure of all the details."

"Would you mind finding out what kind of meat it is and then calling us back?" he asks hesitantly.

"What do you mean, 'What kind of meat?' It's meat, Edgar. It's food. Why should it matter?" I ask.

"Well, it does matter, Beth. Would you mind calling me back when you know?"

So I dial Todd and, exasperated, ask, "What *kind* of meat is it? Edgar wants to know."

"Oh, Beth, you won't believe it. It's the best meat money can buy — steak and incredible cuts of beef and pork. They're going to love it."

So I call Edgar back to report.

"Praise God!" he breathes into the phone; then he asks me to hold, as he shouts out to the children that the Lord's response to their prayer is on its way over.

Those children prayed that day with the faith of a mustard seed (do you know what the faith of a four-year-old orphan looks like?), and the mountain moved.

And it's still moving.

That night with Joel was a turning point in my faith. I was headed down a path where God and I were working together to meet the needs of abandoned children, but it was working, really, at a pretty low-grade level. I knew how to ask what needs people had, and I had learned how to ask those who had resources to help us meet those needs — and there were lots of days when we could draw a line between the two and I fell into bed with a sense of self-righteousness that God and I were quite the team.

I'm learning to let my back get pushed against a wall — because that is when I cry out for my Rescuer. Most days when I see the wall coming, I angle myself so I don't get anywhere near it. I decide not to say something that I should or not to take a risk that I've been dying to take. I realize now, more than three decades into my life, that the only new things I try tend to be those I'm already good at or capable of. I'm slowly learning to get in over my head, so God can save the day — or at least pick up the pieces. I want to take risks so that I can't bail myself out, so that I am even more grateful when God shows up. Sometimes he not only shows up, but he shows off his supernatural agenda to save the day. Still, more often than not, I learn even more when he simply teaches me again and again the fundamental lesson that his ways are nothing like mine.

He is consistent but hardly predictable. You can pray for healing for four people, and only one might get better. For every story of a Joel being provided with meat, hundreds of people die of hunger. When someone dies in spite of our prayers, or when something doesn't happen that we prayed for, we tend to believe that God doesn't always come through. We get good at explaining to children and new believers why bad things happen to good people anyway, why there's evil in the world, and why "our guy" doesn't always win.

But I'm slowly learning to refuse to be tripped up by such things. When troubles approach, I used to always plan an escape route, thinking that it would keep both God and me from looking bad. But he doesn't require any such excuses. The more childlike and less mature my faith becomes, the easier it is to invite God to come.

Never again will I offer up an explanation that spins God as weak or passive. If God doesn't come through in the way I want him to, it should expand my view of faith, not shrink it. It means there is something else going on, something I can't see or understand, and I have the opportunity to be swept up in it or not.

I am walking toward a more reckless faith. It is not defined by my denomination; its doctrine is constantly in flux as my understanding of how he moves in this world grows. Some days, my faith even feels downright dangerous. Am I allowed to think *that* about God? Can I ask *that* of him? I think he is more fascinated with our dialogue than disapproving of my missteps. I am sure I have them; I can question and push as well as any middle child. But our relationship feels dynamic.

I grew up near an amusement park, and as soon as I turned sixteen I applied to work on the "biggest, fastest, longest wooden roller coaster in the world." I knew everything there was to know about "The Beast" and rode it a dozen times a day for a couple of summers. Even though I could anticipate every turn, what always got me was the feeling in my stomach right before I went down the first hill. Riding 70 mph on a wooden roller coaster twelve times a day sounds like foolishness now, but I don't want to ever outgrow the yearning to feel that alive.

I changed with Joel that night. Now I'm on a path where God does what he does and simply uses me to accomplish his plan when he sees fit. And it is working at breakneck speed. There are more days than not when the lines aren't clear, but more needs are being met than I could have ever have met by myself. Like that roller coaster, it still takes my breath away.

God's provision for orphans reminds me of a great story about Elijah recorded in 1 Kings 17:8 – 24:

Then the word of the Lord came to him: "Go at once to Zarephath of Sidon and stay there. I have commanded a widow in that place to supply you with food." So he went to Zarephath. When he came to the town gate, a widow was there gathering sticks. He called to her and asked, "Would you bring me a little water in a jar so I may have a drink?" As she was going to get it, he called, "And bring me, please, a piece of bread."

"As surely as the Lord your God lives," she replied, "I don't have any bread — only a handful of flour in a jar and a little oil in a jug. I am gathering a few sticks to take home and make a meal for myself and my son, that we may eat it — and die."

Elijah said to her, "Don't be afraid. Go home and do as you have said. But first make a small cake of bread for me from what you have and bring it to me, and then make something for yourself and your son. For this is what the Lord, the God of Israel, says: 'The jar of flour will not be used up and the jug of oil will not run dry until the day the Lord gives rain on the land.'"

She went away and did as Elijah had told her. So there was food every day for Elijah and for the woman and her family. For the jar of flour was not used up and the jug of oil did not run dry, in keeping with the word of the Lord spoken by Elijah.

If we trust God, he will care for us. Imagine how the widow's heart swelled knowing that God looked down into her home and saw *her* and her situation. He asked her to have a reckless faith and trust in a man she had never met, to give away all she had left. When she walked out on that limb, God did more than catch her from falling; he lifted her up and provided for her as the head of her household. Do you remember the God who not only shows up but shows off? Read on to see what he did for this woman's son:

Some time later the son of the woman who owned the house became ill. He grew worse and worse, and finally stopped breathing. She said to Elijah, "What do you have against me, man of God? Did you come to remind me of my sin and kill my son?"

"Give me your son," Elijah replied. He took him from her arms, carried him to the upper room where he was staying, and laid him on his bed. Then he cried out to the Lord, "O Lord my God, have you brought tragedy also upon this widow I am staying with, by causing her son to die?" Then he stretched himself out on the boy three times and cried to the Lord, "O Lord my God, let this boy's life return to him!"

The Lord heard Elijah's cry, and the boy's life returned to him, and he lived. Elijah picked up the child and carried him down from the room into the house. He gave him to his mother and said, "Look, your son is alive!"

Then the woman said to Elijah, "Now I know that you are a man of God and that the word of the Lord from your mouth is the truth."

Did she doubt God's provision and protection after that? Maybe on some days when she, like all of us, let her thoughts get the best of her. But I have a hunch she told more than a few people about how her son's life was saved; maybe she even invited them in for some bread. That's what happens when God meets your need; you can't shut up about it.

Reckless faith is stunning. It is the stuff stories are told about years later. God is calling us to give to others recklessly because that is *his* nature. He could have atoned for our sins many other ways, or just kept accepting our livestock on the altar, but he demonstrated the ultimate in reckless giving when he offered his body for us.

The story of Joel is just one among millions of stories about how God responds to someone's cry each day. He is doing more than fetching what we ask; he is orchestrating events that are multipurpose. He is blessing the receiver, the provider, the asker, the observer, the second-hand hearer; he is big and alive and dynamic and involved. He is a God who captivates me. He is wilder than I can contain, and my understanding of him, while growing each day, only allows me to see a fraction of his total existence.

I remember when I was about six years old having my mouth washed out with soap — not because I'd said a bad word or been sassy to my mother. I had simply said the one word that can still make her wild: *bored*. On rainy days or summer evenings or during long programs designed for adults, we were not allowed to say, "This is boring" or "I'm bored." If she even thought she smelled those words coming, she would quietly remind me that my attitude was what I made of it. If I was bored, it was because I was boring. There were easily a thousand things she could (and would) name that I could do. She was on a mission that we not see life (or her) as a source of entertainment. Life was what we made of it.

Although I've since teased her about all this, she was right. If God bores us, it is we who are boring. He came to give us life to the full. He is infinite and wild. He is fascinating and crying out for us to participate in a life he has designed specifically for us.

Will we fashion him into something he is not but we can easily explain, or will we let him be what we cannot understand, but are drawn to?

Many times I've told Joel that God has big plans for his life. To teach a preschooler that his prayers are heard, and that those prayers move the same hand of God that created the mountains Joel looks at every day, is a mighty heady lesson for a four-year-old.

It is, in fact, a mighty heady lesson for me as well. I often don't see God provide meat in my life because I already have a plan in place to secure it, and more often than not it doesn't involve consulting the Lord. Had Edgar gone that day to humans to provide for his children, he would most likely have received money to buy beans and rice and eggs and tortillas. There's nothing wrong with eating those, and the children would have been grateful, but there is something otherworldly about a King who provides banquet food for his children.

How often do I settle for beans, when, if I had only trusted him, I might have been given steak?

Four

Carolina and Lupita

When I first met them, Carolina was three years old and Lupita was one — and they stole my heart. We had just moved to Mexico, and they lived in one of the orphanages we served. Baby Lupita was underweight, with huge brown eyes, and Carolina had the strongest will I have ever encountered. Since I had no children yet, they quickly became my own life-sized baby dolls. I have hundreds of pictures from that time. On most afternoons I found myself most comfortable with one of them on my hip.

One day, feeling brave, Todd and I sit down with the director of their children's home, and Todd says, "Beth and I would like you to check Carolina and Lupita's next-of-kin regarding adoption."

"The situation is complicated," the director warns, speaking slowly, "since their mother has lost her rights.

Lupita, age five

She's incarcerated, but the father is still available, so don't get your hopes up. I'll mention it to him, however, when he calls next time to see how they're doing."

A month later, the father agrees to begin adoption proceedings, and we can't be more thrilled. By then I am pregnant with my daughter Emma, and I think these three little women will get along perfectly as sisters.

On Christmas Eve the father asks to stop by the orphanage for what we assume will be his last Christmas with his daughters. "Can I have a moment with them alone?" he asks.

"Of course," we concede, and my heart breaks for him. He can't take care of them and has made a difficult decision.

Minutes tick by and we begin to worry. Finally, I can stand it no longer and rush to where they have been sitting.

"Todd!" I cry out, "They're gone!"

Sure enough, the father has jumped on a bus with the girls and broken our agreement.

We pray, "Lord, be with them. Watch over their comings and goings and fill their hearts with what they need. Keep them safe ..." We wonder if we should get in the car and try to find them. But where would we drive to? And what do we do if we find them? We pray constantly in the days and weeks that follow. But by the time spring comes and Emma is born, we are convinced they are gone forever.

A year and a half later, our friend René calls to tell us about a new children's home north of town. "Would you be willing to go and meet with the director?" Since Todd is busy with a visiting team at another children's home, I pack up my toddlers, Emma and Evan, and go check it out. It's a lovely home with three dozen children already. After the director tours us through the dorms, we stop in the kitchen for some water.

"*Gracias*," I tell the woman behind the counter

Carolina and Lupita, the week before they disappeared

51

as she holds a cup in my direction. As I turn to take the cup, I gasp. The cup never makes it to my hand; it falls right through my shaking fingers. "Lupita!"

The director is confused by my reaction, as is the little girl who last saw me when she was only a year old. Paying no attention to the water I've spilled all over me, I kneel down to embrace the toddler. I am sure this is a miracle. In a city of millions, God brings me right to her. Awkwardly she hugs me back. I don't even mind that she has forgotten — because I hadn't. Carolina remembers me, however, and after rounding the corner, she buries herself in my arms. Oh, praise God! Praise God! I am sure I won't be leaving this afternoon without them.

"We tried to adopt them," I explain, breathless. "They were taken … If you would just help us find their father, I think he'd reconsider. He obviously can't take care of them."

"I will not contact anyone until I know you better," she asserts firmly. She *is* their advocate, I realize, and I reluctantly leave the home that afternoon without the girls, but with a heart full of new hope.

Six months later, the director of the girls' orphanage is calling: "Beth, I thought you'd want to know — the girls' father was killed last night. I think your adoption dreams have died with him. There's only an aunt left, and she doesn't seem very cooperative."

And so their story takes on another dark chapter, and we spend the next eight years watching them grow and develop from afar. We pray for them, encourage them, photograph them, and celebrate birthdays with them, but the ending I hoped for now seems impossible.

"Beth, it's about Carolina ..." The director of the orphanage calls me one day. "I thought you'd want to know. We're having trouble with her behavior. I've tried, but I just can't control her. Since she's the oldest, and so strong in character, she's influencing the other children. I thought you'd want to know, but I'm going to be moving her out of our home, permanently. If you want to come and say goodbye, you can."

"What about her sister? Is she being moved out too?" I ask.

"No, she hasn't done anything wrong. She can and will stay. They will be separated."

Todd and I pray that night for guidance on whether we should play a role in this situation. We still love them, but the scars of their lives are obvious, and the situation seems bleak. I find it hard to sleep that night and realize I am struggling with wondering if God is big enough to heal them. I know the answer is yes, but still I pray, "Lord, do I have a faith reckless enough to believe you have always had a plan for them?"

I feel him answering back: "Do you have a faith strong enough to want to be a part of my plan?"

We wake up wondering if God stirred our hearts years ago not so that we'd take action then, but so we would take action now.

So, ten years and four months after we thought we'd be their parents, we check both sisters out of the orphanage and bring them home. There are still lingering details that threaten our arrangement. There are vague family members, like the aunt, who stand in the way of our relationship being legalized. But now that there are behavioral issues, she doesn't want them anyway. Regardless of how the state or outsiders may see our relationship, we function inside our little yellow house like a family. Or at least, we wake up daily with that intention.

On their second night at home, I sit down with Carolina and have the conversation I've been dreading for the past twenty-four hours. It is the "chose-to-obey-or-else-you-will-leave" talk. I tell her, "Until now, I've been the fun aunt who brings you presents and takes your picture, but starting today, we are responsible for your safety, so you have some serious new boundaries."

She just sits there, crying, rocking back and forth. I wonder what she's feeling. I hate not being able to say, "I am in this forever; no matter what you do or say, you can't push me away," but that is simply not the truth. I love her like that, but not only do we have to think about the rest of the family, but she needs to hear that there is some behavior we will not tolerate.

I sit there feeling helpless, knowing her behavior is the direct result of choices others made for her, and I want to make her feel loved and protected, not threatened. This is not going how I hoped.

I grab her chin and stare into her beautiful tear-stained eyes, "But we have *wanted* you for ten years. We have wanted and prayed for you since you were a toddler with an iron will. You were only at that first orphanage for six months, and you know why? So two young married kids could come and fall in love with you. God has been writing your story for a long time, and *this* is the next chapter." Her tears start again, but her eyes change. She is hearing me, or at least listening. "Do you know how many calls we get about children who are being kicked out of orphanages or disciplined or have left? Guess how many of those we invite in our home? None. You are different. This is God finishing what he started long ago. I have no idea why. Now we get to watch why it is so important to him that we live like a family."

I have been so worried about how I can bring Christ to her, share with her a message she has never fully understood. I tossed and turned the previous two nights, struggling with the nagging questions about whether I can give her what she needs. Besides being a mother, I am a missionary, and I'm supposed to carry the gospel with me, right?

As we sit in our back garden, she cries, and I feel the Holy Spirit pursuing her through me. I realize I don't have to muster up anything. I don't need to *carry* the gospel anywhere. It's already everywhere. God has not been passively involved. Suddenly I know that I am his foray into the situation. He isn't relying on me to literally carry his presence — he has been present in her life all along. All I need to do is just *reflect* God so Carolina can see him more clearly, with flesh on. And the best way I can think to do that is through love.

I can lie awake all night wondering about all the questions I have: How does this affect our other children? How can I get these girls to trust us? What happens if it doesn't work out? How much is that going to hurt? Why didn't they get to come and stay earlier? I can spin myself into the darkness with all the fears that surface. But I have seen the view from the limb I am now out on. It's breathtaking, and although the wind today seems a bit strong and both hands are holding on, I have the feeling that one day I will be dancing on that branch with my hands waving over my head. That feeling, that rush that comes from trusting in a God you cannot see but totally believe is there, is worth all the questions my mind and the Enemy can throw at me.

As I write this, I'm afraid. Do I have what it takes to be there for them?

I already know the answer is no — hence, my fear. We've had some bumps in our short new road together. Those bumps are designed to flatten my tires and throw me off course. It is tempting to pull over at the next rest stop, believe me.

Last night I sneaked into their room and watched them sleep. They are so innocent, so vulnerable. They want to be what we want them to be, and they are trying so hard.

I want to be what they need me to be, and I am trying so hard—but will all our efforts be enough? I hope so, but I'm not sure.

So I go back to my original question: Do I believe God has a plan?

Absolutely. And farther out onto the proverbial wobbly limb we all go.

FIVE

The Deposit

Naomi and I are painting our nails again on the steps of the old stone chapel. It is the fourth coat of red for each of us. It is something we can do together without talking, and we like being together. I already know her favorite color (red), her age (twelve), and her name. The only thing left in my Spanish repertoire is the Four Spiritual Laws. It's a hot, August afternoon, and we have nothing but time on our hands. *Just do it already, Beth!*

"Naomi," I start. She looks up from my nails, curious. "Do you know Law One? That God loves you and has a wonderful plan for your life?"

She just shrugs her shoulders, and gives me a look that is part smirk, part annoyance, like she knows something I don't and not the other way around.

I quickly go back to painting her nails and pray to God for another shot.

Although that law is completely true, in the face of her circumstances, it will take some convincing. I realize after spending an entire week focusing on her and only noticing a slight change, sharing with orphans is going to be much more involved than I anticipated.

In our U.S. culture of pulled-up bootstraps and endless American-dream stories, it's easy to believe that the wonderful plan might result in a happy life after three clicks of your heels. And although I do believe that God has a wonderful plan for our lives, I realize now more than ever that it's more about what happens internally due to our involvement with him than a change in our circumstances.

Later that same fall, while hosting a team from the States, I try to explain why we invited them. "We need help with the children's hearts. There is nothing for the gospel to be planted in. We don't just need to cultivate the soil; we need to add soil so the seed has someplace to take root."

I look around the room and wonder if they hear me. Do they realize we have invited them here to paint fingernails?

I grab a piece of paper and begin.

"Imagine that this piece of paper is the heart of an orphan. Every one of them has been abandoned or abused. There is no exception. For some, they don't remember the day they were dropped off; they just slowly grew up with the realization that they lived differently than the other children in the village, school, or on TV. For others, however, they do remember the moment they were left behind, and usually it starts with a lie. They are told they are going to a fair or a carnival, so they skip off the bus or jump out of the taxi and run toward the other children. It's the only way to physically move a nine-year-old. No kid would get on the bus if he knew he was going to an orphanage. Then sometime later on that night, it hits them.

"If you're the oldest child, you feel suddenly responsible and wonder from that moment on how your little brother or sister is eating or sleeping or doing in school. A weight not designed to be carried by a child has been placed on his shoulders. I was talking to a group of girls the other day who were sharing their 'first day' memories. Some of them can go back to as early as two years old and remember what they were wearing, who first picked them up, what they ate. The impact of that first day is so strong, they'll never forget it.

"Whenever that first moment of abuse or abandonment happens, it's like ripping a heart in half." I rip the paper. "Then, after that first rip, more start coming.

"You are the orphan kid in school [rip]. You aren't invited to someone's birthday party [rip]. You don't feel good and no one cares [rip]. It's your birthday and no one remembers [rip]. It's visitation day and no one comes to visit [rip]. It's visitation day and someone comes to visit you, but they only end up walking away [rip]. You don't

61

play sports in school or go to school plays because there isn't anyone to pay the fees or cheer you on or pick you up [rip].

"Sometimes the rips happen because of the treatment you receive from other children or workers within the home [rip]. Sometime it comes from children at school who don't want to sit with you [rip] or it comes on a holiday when you see families laughing together [rip]. Other rips come from punishments you receive that you didn't deserve [rip], or from words that replay in your minds that were carelessly spoken [rip]. Sometimes it comes from adults who sense you are an easy prey and come back to hurt what is already considered damaged goods [rip].

"With each rip the heart gets smaller and smaller and harder and harder, so it's no wonder that when I told that girl, 'God loves you and has a wonderful plan for your life,' she gave me a look that said, 'Great plan. I don't want anything to do with a God who had *this* in mind.'"

Looking at the confetti now strewn around the room, I look up and confess, "I wonder most days, 'What can we do now? How can we possibly get started?'"

My voice is thick with emotion now, "I don't have the answer, but I *do* know it will take more than me to do it."

I look up and meet their eyes. "Thanks for just showing up."

There are 143.5 million orphans in the world. If I focus on the staggering numbers, I will never take any action. It would stun anyone into inactivity, just the way the statistics about hunger and aborted babies and AIDS in Africa do. So what can I possibly do to fight the tide?

When I simply ask myself how I can make a deposit in the life of one child today, I feel creative, alive, and swept up into the movement of the Creator who is pursuing with a holy passion "the least of these." We cannot solve the orphan problem. Jesus said the poor would always be among us, and as long as there is poverty and disease, there will be orphans. If I thought we had to solve the orphan problem, I would spend all my days pushing that train uphill.

Instead, I am going to join God, or come behind him, as he is the Father to the fatherless and uses me as an extension of his holy hand. I love to hear about other ministries and people in other parts of the world who are doing what we are doing. I don't want to be the only or the biggest or even the best at reaching orphans.

I sometimes hear people say that their ministry is unique, that no one is doing what they are doing. Shouldn't that be a red flag? Of all the believers in the world, is it possible they are tuned into a channel that no one else can hear?

Somehow God is reaching out to 143.5 million orphans. I don't know how he is doing it in Indonesia or China or Mozambique, but I know how he is doing it in Monterrey, Mexico, and I want to be his vessel here.

We're often asked, "How do you deal with so much heartbreak? Aren't you sad all the time?" The answer is complicated, and each person answers differently, but ultimately all of us believe at some level the story isn't over. There is more to be written; it is a story full of hope and redemption. If I believed God was only loosely involved, passively observing as we and others make a mess of our lives, I would feel desperate about this state of affairs. But I believe in a God who is intricately woven into the soul of each person he knit together, and he has written chapters we have yet to read. Most days my role in the kingdom is as complicated as painting fingernails. It's usually just about showing up.

One of my first lessons in reckless faith in Mexico came from a man named Pepe. He and his wife, Lucy, became believers in adulthood. They had children, a house, and employment. Many evenings, as they watched the nightly news together, they would hear reports on crimes committed in an area downtown called La Coyotera. One evening a newscaster reported that even the police were afraid to go into this community, and as a result, it was a favorite hangout for criminals.

Pepe decides he can't watch the news anymore. He has to take action. He takes a bus into the *centro* and sits down in a bar in the heart of La Coyotera.

When he returns home later that evening, he is so excited — not that anything happened there that night, but he knows that he felt a rush in his spirit and a desire to return. And return he does, night after night, and he begins sharing his faith with the men in the bar and outside on the streets. Eventually, he strikes up a relationship with the bar owner, whom he leads to the Lord. One night while they're talking, the bar owner asks Pepe, "What would you do if you had this building?"

Pepe, in a common pose

"What do you mean?" Pepe asks.

"I mean, if this wasn't a bar where men could come and forget about their problems. What would you *do* here for the men in this community? How would you help them forget about their lives and struggles?"

Pepe promises to pray about that question and goes home to share it with his wife.

Less than a year later, on the site where Pepe had first come to see La Coyotera up close, he opens a mission. In the morning, men come to receive a hot breakfast while they hear Pepe share about not forgetting their lives, but finding true purpose in Jesus Christ.

Good news travels fast, and Pepe's mission is no exception. Already he is starting to outgrow his little building. A group of formerly homeless and jobless men are now working for him, making food, cleaning up the building, following up with people who visit. They function much like an elder board.

A man in La Coyotera finding peace

By the time we meet Pepe on his street corner, with a big black Bible in his hands, his mission occupies most of the city block. He has a church across the street from the original mission and a home where men and women can get the help they need to break free from drug addiction.

I love going to Pepe's church. Most days he has "open mike" — and there are some R-rated testimonies. God saves prostitutes, gang members, deadbeat dads, and gluesniffers in droves. I've never asked Pepe when this motley crew began to get together or how many of them might have grown up in an orphanage (or should have grown up in one). Statistics say 90 percent of orphans go into the black market or into prostitution. They often lack the family support and sometimes the moral compass that would help keep them from resorting to illegal activities. Pepe is used to picking up the pieces in the lives of adults who were once broken children.

One night, Zeke, a visiting friend, asks us if his little team can spend the night down at Pepe's mission to help out with the increased number of people who show up there once the sun goes down. I call Pepe. He weighs the risks but says, "If God is calling them to come tonight, it's probably because he has a reason for it."

Our group goes down there to work, serve, pray, and clean. At bedtime Pepe makes sure that the team is settled in for the night; then he goes outside, closes the door behind him, and without drawing any special attention to himself, lays down in front of the church door, and sleeps on the street. If anyone wants to break in and hurt the Americans, they'll literally have to move Pepe first.

Pepe died a few years ago. Old age and a battle against illness finally claimed him. He is now in our great "cloud of witnesses." I know we can't hear those witnesses, but their lives still tell us amazing stories. Noah's story teaches us to listen even when what we hear doesn't make sense. Abraham's story says that our God is always "on time." And Pepe's story tells us that it is always important to take the first step because that's how every journey starts.

Some of those who heard Pepe preach were able to take their first steps out of addiction; others heard him and took their first steps toward reconciliation. When I heard him, he encouraged me to take my first steps toward a dream even when I could only imagine it in part.

Pepe could have lived the last two decades of his life in greater luxury — with more security and fewer complications — and he would still be in heaven and in communion with God. But I can hear him saying, "Betty [that's what he called me], keep one foot in eternity. This world is not our home."

He made deposits in the lives of hundreds of people whose lives are now different because Pepe lived a reckless faith. He breathed spiritual confidence into those around him. He was not a great preacher, nor was he able to pray eloquently. He was not a gifted fundraiser for his mission. Another person might have been great at all those things and still had a lackluster ministry, bearing little fruit and encouraging complacency. But Pepe was good at one essential thing: he trusted that God had a purpose for his life. As a result, God took care of the rest. There were always tamales for the morning outreach, and there were always people who came to hear him preach — all because one night he shut off the TV and walked into a bar.

Hardly the stuff we learn about in Sunday school!

So as I hold up these torn pieces of paper for our guests, I tell them they are going to play a part in a plan that God had since the beginning of time. It is God who is in pursuit of the orphaned child, and he is using them to send his message. It's the same message that he sends to a broken man, addicted and homeless, and the same message that captivates us. This message is so amazing that we don't need to worry or work at shoving it down anyone's throat or to regulate it with a bunch of mandatory meetings.

God has already made some tremendous promises to orphans in Scriptures. Our only goal is to take the pieces that have been ripped and deposit them back into their hearts.

> Not in our name,
>> or in the name of our church,
>> or in the name of our ministry
>> or in the name of the Church.
> We are to make deposits in the name of Jesus.

When faced with a twelve-year-old girl whose heart has been ripped to pieces, you must ask yourself, What would Jesus do at this moment? Would he feel defeated by the statistic that shows that 90 percent of these girls end up in prostitution?

No. I think I know what he'd do. He might not even speak. He might just sit next to her and help her paint her fingernails.

SIX

Gabriela

When I first met Gabriela, she was ten years old, a funny girl with long legs, a knack for speaking English, and a yet-to-be-diagnosed disability. She lived in one of the orphanages where I worked, and although her intensity sometimes made me want to avoid her, the truth is, she is magnetic. Somewhere around age fifteen, after she had repeated fourth grade three times, Gaby left. She went "home" with an uncle who needed help with an ailing aunt. I lost track of her then.

One day, years later, I answer the phone. "Beth," a voice whispers. The rest is inaudible until the line goes dead.

"Who was that?" I wonder. "Bad connection? Someone nervous, shy?"

The next day, same time, another call. "Beth, this is Gaby," but she's still talking too low for me to understand her.

I make a connection with her name but wonder why she is not speaking more loudly and clearly. I don't have long to wait.

The third day, I'm expecting her call. "Gaby," I practically shout into the phone. "Where are you? Where've you been?"

She answers me with screams and fits of rage. I can hear now why she had been using such restraint. Months after arriving at her aunt and uncle's, her aunt died. Struck with grief, her uncle turned her out of the house, unwilling to handle her care. She had no option but to live for a while under a bridge in a park.

Then one day a man appears and says to her, "Your uncle told me I could find you here. Would you like to come to my house and work for me, in exchange for a bed and food?"

In what she assumes is a wonderful stroke of luck, she moves in with the man's family that same day. What she doesn't know is that her uncle can't pay his bills, so he has offered the doctor Gaby instead.

At first it's like a dream — she cooks and cleans, and in exchange is given a bed, a roof, and a toilet. That dream, however, turns into a nightmare when the man begins to visit her bedroom at night, and after each violent episode, he gives her a tiny pill to swallow.

One night he forgot the pill, and on that evening she conceived his son.

"The night my son was born," she explains, "the nurse realized I was alone. She lied to me and turned my baby over to social services after saying she wouldn't."

I try to comfort Gaby and gently offer, "Still, the nurse probably saved his life, because you were alone, Gaby."

She describes her feelings after the baby was born, when they were left alone together in the room. She can't quite put a name to her feelings but just kept saying they were powerful. I say, "Gaby, that's *love*. What you were feeling was *love*." She's shocked. That baby is the purest kind of love she has ever felt.

So she's calling me now because she wants my help getting her baby back.

"Gaby," I say, "why don't you come here for awhile and live on our campus? Your situation is complicated. I'm not even sure how I'd help you get custody — or even if it's a good idea."

After Gaby arrives at our campus, we sit down that first afternoon, and I look at her and confess that there are no easy answers. We begin by reading some of the promises God has made to orphans in Scripture. There are so many, but he specifically promises to vindicate orphans and rescue them; to deliver them and not to leave them; to come to them, hear them, and lift them up; to be their Father and make them a home and lead them out. He says he will not forget them, that he will extend mercy towards them and execute true justice. He will provide them with food and clothing and be their helper, and he will maintain their cause and incline his ear.

After reading each of those passages slowly, I say, "Gaby, I believe his Word is true; it's not a fairy tale or a false promise. It is not poetry or someone else's idea of how we should live. It's the living Word of God, and I'm confident that we can trust God to move in this situation. I'm just not sure how or when or where or in what way, but I know that we can ask God to show up, and he will remind us that he's already here. He has a plan."

Gaby knows at which government orphanage her baby is being held, so for more than a month, she stands outside the building every day and talks about her son to the people coming in and out. Consequently, she learns the names of the workers there, and they, in turn, learn who she is.

Then one July afternoon, months after her arrival, I hear a knock at the door. Three nervous women from Gaby's son's orphanage are standing in the doorway.

"Please don't tell anyone we're here," says one of the women nervously, "but Gaby's parental rights are going to be severed tomorrow at five o'clock. I just thought she should know what's coming. I don't know what you can do in a day, but after tomorrow, she won't be able to decide what happens to her son. We want to tell her so at least she knows what to expect." The women seem relieved and leave quickly.

When Gaby hears the news, she falls on the floor, crying, and she asks me over and over why we haven't tried to do something sooner. Struggling not to panic, I begin to pray.

"Gaby, listen," I say. "What are your options, really? You can't raise the baby all by yourself because you can't offer a stable environment. Honey, I know we've been avoiding this conversation, but your only choice is to give him up for adoption."

Because of the bureaucracy and the number of forms and signatures required, adoptions in Mexico are challenging to say the least, and there seems to be no way we can get the ball rolling before five o'clock the next day — especially since we don't even have a couple willing to adopt the boy.

Once again we read through God's promises for orphans. I tell Gaby, "You know what? I don't know how or what it might be, but I know that your Daddy has a plan, your Father in heaven is working right now on that plan, and we just need to surrender to it."

Then I have a thought. I call a Mexican couple from our church in Monterrey, knowing that they've been disappointed many times in their attempts to adopt a child. I explain the situation to them and ask them to take one more risk, to walk out to the end of a shaky limb with Gaby and me — just for one day — and see what God might have in store for them.

The next day, Friday, when we arrive at the government facility, Gaby is on one side of me, shaking, crying, and chanting, "Daddy's got a plan, Daddy's got a plan ..." On my other side is the woman from our church, who is standing there, fearful, afraid to trust God, this girl, the adoption system, or that there might be a blessing for her in all of this. We are quite a sight as we shuffle toward the security window.

After checking in, we walk around the corner to wait in what is always an extremely long line to see the social worker, which is only the first of many stops we have to make this day. But as we round the corner, I stop short and stare. There, all in a row, are the social worker, the lawyer, the clerk of courts, the notary, and the psychologist — all the people necessary to process an adoption. Never before have I seen all these key players in the same room, and definitely not assembled on such short notice. "I didn't know you all knew each other!" I quip. They all laugh nervously.

"Daddy *does* have a plan," I whisper to myself, as we begin to move through the rest of the day, filling out forms, getting signatures, being interviewed. Here we are, on a Friday afternoon, and person after person is able to clear their schedules to make time to help this simple nineteen-year-old girl give up the most important person in her life.

When we are standing in the last office, they bring Gaby's son up from the nursery so Gaby can say goodbye to him. The nurse wisely hands him first to Gaby. She awkwardly holds him and puts her face right next to his.

"I am sorry I was born this way," she tells him. "I am sorry I don't have a mama to help take care of you. I am sorry I won't see you again ..." Then she leans closer and whispers in his ear, "But our Daddy has a plan." Her voice falters at first but grows stronger as she continues. "He has a plan to rescue you. He has a plan to come to you. He has a plan to hear you. He has a plan to make you a home ... He has a plan."

Then she kisses his cheek and hands him over.

Gaby's life didn't suddenly fill with sunshine that day. Doing the right thing, even when it is God's will, isn't a ticket to happiness. Gaby's grieving process will be long and especially complicated by her history and special needs. But she has peace.

Nor did my life or the adoptive parents' lives fill with sunshine either. We continue to meet unexpected obstacles that keep us from bringing the adoption to conclusion. In light of how smoothly everything went on that Friday, the judge in the case is having problems believing that everything was done legally. It was just so remarkable.

I am the kind of person who always wants the pieces to fit perfectly together, but these days, I admit, they don't seem to. Still, I refuse to fall into despair. Despite the continuing obstacles, I was there with Gaby that day, and I saw God do miracles. He has his reasons for doing what he does — reasons that he promises will be the right thing for the adoptive parents, for the baby, and for Gaby. Daddy has a plan. Though the final chapter is not yet written, I know no matter how the adoption is resolved, no weapon formed against God's will can prevail.

So I wait and hope.

Sometimes reckless faith requires no further action. You just have to hold on to the limb you've been led out on and trust that it doesn't break.

SEVEN

Caleb

The phone rings. I reach for it, then hesitate. For a moment I consider letting the answering machine pick it up, since it is a Friday afternoon at 5:00 — my least favorite time to deal with incoming calls.

Get it, a voice seems to nudge me. I grab it an instant before the machine answers.

"Beth?" says a voice on the other end. "It's Sandra. I work at one of the local orphanages. I'm glad I caught you. We have a young girl here who has a newborn baby she wants to drop off this afternoon, but she doesn't have any paperwork. I can't accept her son until Monday morning when we get him a birth certificate, but I am afraid if I send her back out in the streets, we won't see her again. Can she and her baby stay with you for the weekend?"

Truthfully, a small battle rages inside me. I'm aware that the favor she's asking of me will take a toll on our weekend plans, but then again, these calls are the very reason I live here. So I agree.

Fifteen minutes later, they're at the door.

"Okay. Well, here she is, and this is Caleb," says the social worker as she hands the baby over to me. I can hardly disguise my shock when I see how young this new mother is. She's fourteen.

I lead her down the hall. "Here's your room." I point to one of the doors. As she settles in, I try to figure out how to penetrate her detached attitude. She doesn't seem to care about anything, she isn't easily impressed with anything, and she doesn't laugh at my jokes. This is going to be a long weekend.

"Do you want me to bathe your baby? Would you like him to sleep with us tonight?" At last she seems grateful. After weeks of caring for her baby without anyone's help, she hands him over to me; then, completely exhausted, she falls asleep.

I stand in her doorway, watching her sleep, and I wonder what is going on in her heart. She thought she would have to give her baby up forever today, but now she has two more days to spend with him. Is she happy? Frustrated? Scared?

In the morning I am full of questions: "Who is the baby's father? Where are your parents? Where do you live? What are your plans?" Her answers are curt and tense. Her body language tells me to leave her alone. So I turn my attention from the difficult mother to the adorable baby, who, in contrast to his mother, melts in my arms and turns toward my body when I hold him.

I know God's many promises to orphans and I feel confident he has his eye on this little one. God led him to my door, hadn't he? He must have a plan.

"Caleb," I whisper in his ear, "God is dreaming up a wonderful life for you and a future full of hope." It feels so eternal and is exactly why I had become a missionary to orphans, so I could rock them and tell them about God's love. I am alternating between these precious moments with Caleb, and then I look up and see his mom, and the mood shifts.

She is sassy, hard, and not easily engaged.

"Did you sleep okay?" I ask.

"Whatever."

"You hungry?"

"Whatever."

"We have all day; what would you like to do?

"I don't know. Whatever."

In the early afternoon, when I discover the baby has severe diaper rash and is malnourished, I struggle with judgmental feelings. How could this girl have let him get this way? *Lord, in all the hours she's cared for him today, did she never once change his diaper?* I certainly won't whisper anything like that in her ear, however, because she just might bite mine off.

Thankfully, God, who has started a good work in me, will not let me sit quietly in my sin. This weekend, our multifaceted

God has a plan to care for Caleb, initiate healing his mother, and convict me of my bad attitudes.

It takes no effort to look down on people. It's actually a lazy thing to do. When I think of the people I have looked down on in the past, they are usually people whose lives I couldn't relate to. They lived in different times or places, and it was too much work for me to try to understand their point of view. Had God not allowed me to see life through this young mother's eyes later that afternoon, I might still have the question, How did she get herself into this mess?

Around 4:00 that afternoon, I am waiting for some people from another orphanage we work with to come over for a cookout. With Caleb on my hip, I wander into the girl's room and say, "We're having some dinner guests tonight. You don't have to help, but at the least come out and eat with us; it's the only dinner I'm serving tonight."

She maintains her look of disinterest, so I roll my eyes back at her and saunter out, still carrying Caleb.

Then a van pulls up and the kids from the visiting orphanage start to stream out the back.

Caleb's mom has come out of her room and looks like she wants to say something to me, but before she can, the front door of the van opens. As I walk forward to greet the orphanage director, I hear Caleb's mother's gasp behind me. When I turn to see what the problem is, she grabs Caleb out of my arms and runs back to her room. I follow her.

When I reach the room, the door is locked, but I can hear her sobs. I put my head against the door, listen for a moment, and decide to leave her alone.

Soon we start our dinner. When I think I won't be noticed, I slip out and walk quietly back to the girl's room and knock softly. Opening it slightly, she yanks me inside.

"Don't make me go out there," she says, trembling. "I grew up with that lady, and the last thing I want her to know is that she was right. I walked myself right into a trap."

"You grew up at that orphanage?" I ask in disbelief.

"Yes. I left there a year ago, listening to the sweet talk of a boy I met each day after school and walked home with. Only one day, I didn't walk home. We just kept going and by the time I realized I was far from the orphanage, I was filled with such freedom I didn't care. About a month later, they found me and insisted I return. They made all sorts of threats that if I didn't come with them then, I wouldn't be able to come back at all. But, by then I was addicted to what the boy was selling and a month later I was pregnant."

I sit there shocked at what she's telling me. She is an orphan herself. What does it feel like to have no model for a mother and yet to be one yourself? Tears form in my eyes until I can't keep them back. I suddenly realize the same promises about orphans I have been whispering to Caleb also apply to her.

"He stopped showing me off, loving me, once I was pregnant, so now I just clean up the house and make myself useful to whoever I can, if you know what I mean. I don't want this baby to grow up in that environment, and I don't trust what he will do to Caleb if he gets angry at the crying or at me. He doesn't want to be a father, but he is probably going crazy right now because I didn't come home last night. He will wonder where the baby is, and I don't know if even *I* can return there.

"I can't see her," she rambles on until I realize she now means the orphanage director. "She was right, but I can't let her know that. I can't go back there until I have my life straightened out. Please don't tell them I'm here."

In just five minutes' time, she has quadrupled the number of words that she has spoken all weekend, but this new vulnerability cracks the door for me to begin ministering to her. First it requires that I get off my throne of contempt and criticism. Truthfully, it feels much better. Now overwhelmed with the privilege I have to speak truth into a heart so broken, I am convicted beyond words for my judgmental thoughts. It is so easy to judge a mother — but there is, in every case, a back story.

On Monday, we deliver Caleb and his mother to an orphanage where she processes the baby's birth certificate. Today Caleb is just starting to talk, and I still whisper in his ear, not about the mother who gave him up, but about a woman who dreamed something better for him than she could offer herself — the woman who got in over her head and sought out Christians as a refuge for him as they had once been for her.

We don't all start out on the same block. We don't all get the same adults, houses, vacations, educations, in our lives. We don't get the same experiences; we don't have the same capacities or support systems. We generally do the best we can with what we are handed. Even if someone behaves differently than I would, I am still in no position to judge. There are exceptions, but most mothers are goodwilled and genuinely think of the children's home as the best place for provision and protection for their child.

I have carried Caleb's lesson into many circumstances when I want to look down on how dirty a place is or how poorly cared for a child is. I can be tempted to be lazy and think, "Well, I would never have let it get so bad." That is first of all an assumption I cannot make, and secondly, it's not fair. Only a God who sees our life from the beginning through to the end has the right to judge us, and even he

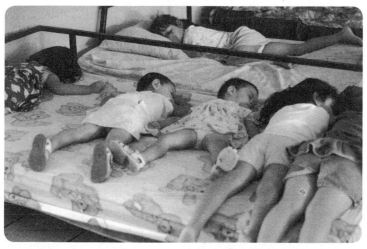

The home where Caleb now lives

doesn't look at the outward appearances. He looks at the heart.

God's promises apply to us all and so does his mercy. Though my faith sometimes wavers, I am hoping that God has Caleb's life in his hands, that he knew Caleb would be safer in the children's home than with his mother. I am hoping Caleb one day will see it that way too. Faith and hope are back to back in the heart of a reckless believer. We hope that the One we have faith in has a plan. And we have faith that that plan will bring us eternal — and earthly — hope.

EIGHT

Running like Jesus

Finally then, brethren, we request and exhort you in the Lord Jesus, that as you received from us instruction as to how you ought to walk and please God (just as you actually do walk), that you excel still more.

Now as to the love of the brethren, you have no need for anyone to write to you, for you yourselves are taught by God to love one another; for indeed you do practice it toward all the brethren who are in all Macedonia. But, we urge you, brethren, to excel still more.

1 Thessalonians 4:1, 9 – 10 NASB, emphasis added

I love to run. It's a moment in my day that belongs just to me, to my thoughts. I sometimes pray, sometimes dream, sometimes noodle a problem, but there was one day in the first week of January a couple of years ago that I could not stop thinking about some friends.

As I run by their house, I look in and see no activity. I pass again, and this time, my heart starts to race because I'm feeling a nudge of concern about them. I basically run in a loop and, although redundant, find comfort in the familiarity of every step. This day, every time I pass their home, I feel an alarm go off. *What is it, Lord?* Finally, as I walk my cool-down lap, I stop (*enough already, Lord!*) and knock.

When they answer the door, I say, still a bit breathless from the run, "I feel kind of silly saying this —" I laugh nervously, and they look at me curiously. I blast ahead, "But I keep praying for you this morning, with urgency. I don't why or for what reason. Maybe something important is coming up in your life." They look concerned, but intent. "Don't worry," I say. "I have the feeling whatever it is will be a blessing."

We take a moment to pray together, and then I walk home.

I'm not sure what it is all about, but I feel better having said something.

Although most of the year we experience extreme heat, this time of year can be bitterly cold. For the month of January, everyone has to get by without heat. It had been 30 degrees the night before and even in our well-sealed home, we slept in our winter coats. For the homeless and those living in poverty, these days can be downright brutal.

Through a friend I've been hearing about a grandmother who is caring for her young grandsons, abandoned by their drug-addicted mother. That grandmother is in poor health, has little money or interest in the long-term care of the children, ages three, two, one, and nine months.

So when the temperatures hit the freezing mark one night, Todd and I commit to looking in on these little boys the next day. In the morning I grab my friend Kate, and we pay her a visit.

On the way there, I tick off items on my to-do list: "I'm thinking about some blankets, maybe a gas-powered space heater; let's get them some food that's easy to heat up ..." But when we arrive, my to-do list looks like a pathetic Band-aid on a serious problem.

With the sense that God is leading us to take bigger steps, we offer to care for the boys temporarily until the older woman's situation — or the weather — changes. Even while making the offer and bundling up the boys, I feel a little rush of adrenaline, an excitement about how God is going to use me, but by the time I turn onto the exit for home, I realize it might not have been the wisest of choices, since my house is already pretty hopping.

The boys, we discover, require a lot of care, especially the nine-month-old, who is clearly developmentally delayed. The back of his head is flat where he has been left lying on a bed for most of his short life.

Sometime into the second week, my family of nine has hit their limit. Toys are scattered everywhere, and we can't walk without stepping on a sippy-cup or a pair of shoes. No one is sleeping well. We call the whole family together, and we invite those friends whose house I regularly jog past, to discuss another plan.

"Please, everyone, pray for a long-term solution. I know God has a plan for these children's lives, but I just don't think it's with Todd and me." I look around at everyone.

Our friends approach us afterward to say they would be willing to take the littlest one — but only for a short time — since he is the hardest by far to care for.

So that night, the baby went home with them — and has never left.

In the year that follows, this family manages to find the birth mother. They get her permission to adopt the baby, finalize their paperwork, raise the necessary funds, and then they wait. When the adoption decree finally comes through, it legalizes what is already clear to everyone who knows them — the boy is their son and was meant to be since the beginning of time.

For most of us who have adopted, that's enough. To take in a child who is not your own is commendable, and to take a child with a special need is remarkable. But this family has a reckless faith, and they are familiar with that verse from First Thessalonians, quoted above, about excelling *still more*.

When Paul wrote to the Thessalonians that they should "excel still more," he was asking a lot from them. They were already doing so much right. They could have responded, "... praying for our enemies, check; risking our lives to worship in public, check; sharing our faith in the face of persecution, check ...," and so on. But Paul exhorts them not to stop. Like them, our goal should be to excel still more in love, always tapping into the endless resources of our Father. We should never make excuses to stop loving, even when people are as hard to love as the birth mom of that abandoned nine-month-old.

Two years have passed since that January morning when our friends first took their son into their home. They have since moved back to the States, and the adoption has long been finalized.

Still, they call me a lot. They usually ask, "Have you heard anything new?" by which they mean, How's the birth mom doing? What's happening with her? "Tell her we're praying for her," they say, "and for her other children. We're hoping for her salvation and advocating for her needs in our church."

The fact is, I *do* hear about the birth mom from time to time and struggle with my critical feelings toward her. She's caught in a cycle of depression and addiction, struggling to make life work and mired in shame about her choices. She's usually unresponsive to our attempts to reach out to her — unless there's something in our hands.

Then one day last October, these same friends come back to Mexico for a visit, and not surprisingly, they want to visit their son's birth mom. Once there, they show her pictures of their son and talk through what most people would avoid, like the painful reality that they see her son wake up every day and she doesn't, that they have this connection because her life went awry. They patiently and relentlessly pursue her heart, answering her questions about God until she has no more.

And in an "only God could have orchestrated it" kind of way, the adoptive parents of her abandoned son lead this woman to the foot of the cross, where she receives full forgiveness for her sins. God has her name written in his Book of Life and used what the Enemy planned for evil (the tossing aside of a human life) to connect them, so they would have a platform from which to speak truth into her life.

The birth mom has since shared with me that when her son was born, she was coming out of a drug-induced haze, but she remembers clearly the doctors telling her that the baby was stillborn. In fact, there is hospital documentation to support her testimony that he was not breathing for several hours. While she was in another room, recovering, God reached down and, I believe, breathed his supernatural breath into that little body, and the baby came back to life.

Her eventual recognition that the child had a special need spiraled her downhill until she could no longer handle his presence and the guilt it brought. So she abandoned him. The burden she carried about his abandonment was *so* heavy that it took someone who understood that part of her life to remove it. But God used her own abandoned son as the key to her understanding how forgiveness works. When she saw that God values every life and each person has a special purpose, it broke her heart and the burden was lifted. She saw before her a new life, an eternal plan, a merciful God, unselfish parents, a boy with a future and a hope and a Savior.

"She did it!" My friends yell as they bound through the door, full of emotion.

"Did what?" I call from the kitchen.

"She accepted the Lord this afternoon. She gets it. She gets adoption into the Kingdom; she gets the idea of forgiveness of sins." They are beside themselves. "It was so great ...," and they proceed to tell me the whole story.

When they finish, I begin, "I'm speechless ..." We look at each other, and I try again. "Yes, of course, you're the perfect people to share grace with her. I just ... I just can't believe you were so willing. Unbelievable. You pursued her."

Just like her Savior.

Still more.

NINE

Isaac

"Go on, fight him," taunts one of the boys.

But I don't want to fight anyone, Isaac thinks; I'm tired of fighting. He backs up against the wall, hoping all the attention will just go away.

"What? You afraid? Where did you come from anyway, that you don't know how to fight?" More than one boy is yelling now, and more of them are gathering around to get a look at the new kid in the orphanage.

As he balls his hands into fists, Isaac thinks, Afraid? Yes. But not of you. I'm afraid I'll hurt you.

They keep taunting him — then BAM! He knocks down the boy who's chanting the loudest and then walks back to get into his new bed. Better to hurt them before they hurt you. He pulls up the covers over his head and thinks about his three little brothers.

That morning his mother told him, "Isaac, go see if it's a good place for me to bring your younger brothers." It is the second children's home that Isaac has been sent to in a year. "You know I need you to check it out first," says him mom, "and you are the strongest. I can't handle it anymore. It's just too much. I'll be back in a month, and I'll be waiting to hear what you have to say. Oh, Isaac — " She stops, and he pauses midstep, waiting to hear what she wants, hoping she'll say something to make this awful situation better. "Never mind," she mutters as she kisses him. Then she walks away.

I will do this for my brothers, he thinks as he falls asleep that night. I'll make everyone here afraid of me so that when my brothers come, they won't be bothered. At eleven, Isaac already feels grown up. He wonders, will it ever get better . . . ?

In some ways it does. His brothers come the following month, and the four of them look out for each other, with Isaac bearing the greatest burden.

When I meet him for the first time about a year later, I notice he's still a pretty sensitive kid, despite his surroundings. He will play with babies and children when other kids his age don't even notice them. But there are other moments when he's tough and hard and difficult to engage.

One night, while walking by the cafeteria in the orphanage where he lives, I see him up ahead, quietly drawing. I'm fascinated by his face. He doesn't know I'm there, and he looks so relaxed, so peaceful. He's leaning against the wall, with his ripped jeans and heavy sweatshirt even though it's warm outside, lost in his notebook. Something about what he's doing or thinking makes his face look different. I should feel guilty about spying on him, but I can't tear myself away. A noise makes him stop. He shoves his drawing into his backpack and looks around.

No one saw you, Isaac, I say silently, as he stands up and his old, bored look returns again. Your secret is safe with me.

And so his life at the children's home drags on, year after year.

"What am I going to do?"

It's July, and time for Isaac's junior high graduation. He needs to make some decisions about his future. We watch him flounder as he tries to figure out what to do. At the graduation ceremony, he looks out at the crowd gathered, and when our eyes meet, I smile.

So what *is* Isaac going to do? I think, as I watch him stand up there in his blue cap and gown. My mind wanders back to a few nights before when he came to visit us. He seems to have only two choices, and since neither of them come close to what God has created him to do, they are equally uninspiring.

"I could leave and get a job," he told us in the kitchen that night, "or I can go to a technical school." You see, neither he nor anyone around him believes he has any more potential than that.

"Everyone tells me I should go to work in a factory," he sighs, "and earn some money. Then I could help my family out ... but I'm not sure what to do — or what I *want* to do."

"Isaac, you know you can stay here with us and continue your studies," Todd says. "Besides, quite selfishly, we'd just love to have you around here some more."

He looks up. "Then I'll enroll at the vocational high school," Isaac says, looking away from us. "I found a school I think I could do okay in."

Isaac (on right) with a staff friend, Matt Cooper

My heart both leaps and sinks. Although happy that he's making a decision and not trying to make it alone, I know he's a gifted and creative artist. I had hoped he'd consider architecture or graphic arts, but his sub-par junior high grades loom in the background. He's a big boy, with a strong stature, and going into "the arts" isn't even on his radar.

While some of the other boys in his class are among our first students to consider a college-preparatory high school program, Isaac gets on his bus every day and shuffles off to high school classes that satisfy other people's expectations for his life but not his own. For a boy with his background, learning a practical skill seems like the "right thing," but it certainly doesn't energize him.

This is how he moves along for the next couple of years.

One day, as his graduation from the tech high school approaches, I say to him, "Isaac, we're so proud of you. But what's next? What do you want to *do* now with your skills?"

He doesn't answer for a long while. Finally he laughs sarcastically. "Nothing," he says. "What do I *want* to do? Draw! That's all I've ever wanted to do. I love commercials and cartoons. I like ads and film and design." His voice begins to pick up and sound animated. "Is there somewhere I can go and study *that*? That's what I *want* to do."

I want to hug him for being honest with himself at last, and I want to slug him for waiting until the week of graduation to admit it.

"Sure there's a place to study that," I respond, "but first you have to go to college-prep high school — that's the track you *didn't* choose two years ago. To do that now means going back into a classroom with fifteen-year-olds, and you'll be eighteen. It means finishing high school, then adding a four-year college degree on top of that. I'm glad you know what you want, but it's a big decision. It's not something you can just start and not finish."

I look at him pleadingly and then plunge ahead: "So do you want it? You have to want it, want it enough that when it's hard, you just do it anyway. It'll take tremendous energy to change your study habits, your expectations of yourself, your capacity to meet new people and be in new environments. You'll have to change your work ethic, change how you spend your time and with whom you spend your time, change how you spend your money and what you value …"

I take a deep breath. I don't want to say all that, knowing it sounds more like a threat, but I need him to understand. "Do you want the big change — the future, a job you love — enough to start with all these daily little changes?"

His big brown eyes look so vulnerable. Then, he drops his fist into his other hand and says, "Yes!"

Isaac has changed tremendously since I first met him. I wonder if change isn't simply becoming more of who you've never been, reversing the world's impact on who God made you to be. Isaac no longer believes everyone is looking for a fight; the wound he experienced that first night in the children's home doesn't have to keep bleeding.

Eventually, his sort of reckless faith grows into actually desiring the upheaval of change. It throws itself toward change, believing the best we can be is still to come.

For Isaac, walking into a school situation in which, over and over again, he had to prove that he deserved to be there was a tremendous change. Every time he faced a challenge (a deadline, a hard professor, a snotty group partner, less money than he wanted for materials), he had a choice: either keep at it or quit. Choosing to stay, day by day, built confidence in himself where before there was only fear. It's the kind of confidence that doesn't have to strike the other guy first. The wound in him is healing.

I've learned that kind of reckless faith from Isaac. It's the kind of faith that takes scary risks, risks that don't necessarily put you in physical danger or look impressive from the outside. For the children I serve, and for many of us, it is far more reckless to believe that God created us with a plan in mind than it is to just try something new. It's downright wild to trust someone with your heart and believe they will love you regardless. And it's far better to change course midstream — the moment you realize you've been steered onto the wrong path — than it is to just stick with the cards you have been dealt.

Isaac's most reckless faith moment came the day he enrolled at the prestigious CEDIM University, which is world renowned for its graphic design program. It was his way of saying aloud that he knew he had a gift and was willing to share it — a far cry from the boy hiding behind the building with his notebook. The old Isaac would have settled for any program where he could finish under the radar. But the maturing, changing, engaging Isaac is ready for yet another risk. His reckless faith carries him to the hardest of all options and will see him through as a CEDIM graduate this year.

Today I'm grateful for a God who had Isaac's whole life in his sight when he deposited a gift in him that lay dormant for years while his courage caught up. I'm grateful for Isaac's sake, and for his future family, and for myself, since my life is much richer because I spend time with him.

Last week I walked up behind a boy at the children's home where Isaac grew up. He's new and about the same age as Isaac was when he arrived. He isn't interested in engaging in conversation, so I just sit there in silence as he starts doodling on a napkin and the scribbles begin to take form.

"Wow, that's really good." I try to look in his eye.

Nothing.

"What are you drawing?" I start again.

Still no response.

"There's a boy I know, who's in college to study drawing. Want me to ask him if he would come over here and draw with you?"

This boy is hardcore — still nothing. I sigh and start to push myself up from the table. Then I remember I have a God who sees a whole life at one time. What seems stony to me is mere potential to God. What needs to happen to this little boy before he can realize he has been created for something more? Oh, Lord, show me the way, I pray silently. I sit there for another minute.

"Did I tell you that he used to live here too?"

The boy's head perks up. "He did?" He's looking at me now. "And he's in college?"

Startled by the power of prayer, I laugh and dive in: "Yes, he did and yes, he is. I'll ask him to come over sometime to tell you about it, if you want."

"I'd like that," he says simply, returning to his drawing.

Reckless faith is funny like that. People, when they see it, either criticize it or throw themselves toward it. For my new little friend, I can only hope that Isaac's story, as he gets to know it, will do the same for him as it has for many other children.

Isaac's life makes it easier for us to believe.

Maria and Adriana

Faith is the gas that makes your spiritual journey go.

How reckless can your faith actually get? It's measured by the extent to which you really believe God's plan for you is the best. It requires the kind of faith that believes God's words are not empty promises meant for someone else. It's the kind of faith that says, "Everything will work out in the end" — even if "the end" is eternity.

Over and over again God teaches me that for those with reckless faith, the story is never over. It's childish to throw in the towel, pout, get frustrated, or walk away. Life isn't a puzzle that's too hard or a toy you can't figure out. But so often, I'm tempted to lose faith when I'm confronted with a setback.

When I relax my control on the plotline of my life and give in to the journey God has prepared for me, I lose myself in all the great stories swirling around me. When I stomp my feet and say, "That's not fair!" or "It wasn't supposed to happen that way!" then I run out of gas, and my spiritual journey stalls.

But God is teaching me, one child at a time, that he is the Author of life and can redeem and write any story he wants.

Maria is a young girl who was born with a chip on her shoulder. That chip was put there by the father she never knew, by the mother who preferred her own pursuit of religious activities to her daughter, and by everyone who turned a blind eye to her abusive stepfather. All that dysfunction paved Maria's road to the orphanage, and by the time I knew her, she had a beautiful smile, a bright mind — and an elephant-sized attitude problem.

One night, while at the movies with Todd, I get a sense that something's wrong at home. A beep on my "mom radar," Todd calls it. "Just call home and check it out," he encourages me.

"*Bueno.* Hey, it's me. Is Maria home yet from English class?" I ask my daughter who answers the phone. *I am sure she's fine*, I think, as she searches the house for Maria.

"No, she isn't back yet from class," comes the answer. "Wasn't she supposed to be home hours ago?"

"Yes, she was. That concerns me. We'll head home, but if you hear from her first, call me back, will you?"

We leave the theatre and set out to look for her. At this point, we are more worried that something has happened *to* her than because of her, and we make calls to her friends and pray as we drive between school and home. I'm a cup half-full person, always giving the benefit of the doubt, looking for the silver lining — all the time believing that Maria hasn't done something she knows she shouldn't, or at least on purpose.

Later that night we find her — in the backseat of an old car with a man twice her age. I'm crushed.

Not long after that, Maria leaves us, unable to live within the boundaries we have set for our children.

I don't hear from her for several months. Then, one night, she shows up bleeding and barely clothed. She has walked — barefoot — all the way down the unpaved road to our home. Someone runs to get me, and as I approach her, she calmly says that she had been bully-whipped with a cement block by her pimp who had been angry with her.

As I clean up what should be painful abrasions, I'm struck by the fact that she doesn't flinch; she doesn't seem to feel any pain. "Doesn't this hurt?" I ask.

"Not really."

I'm amazed at how still she sits as I treat her cuts and bruises. "How can this not hurt? These are rocks in your face!"

"I don't feel anything physical anymore," she says. "I haven't for a long time." After her first few "tricks," she explains to me, she stopped feeling anything when anyone touched her.

One day when I was about seventeen, my dad and I go on a daddy-daughter date in his Mustang convertible out on Route 22 & 3, toward what was then farming country. We eat Dilly Bars and breeze past the white picket fences. My dad points out that the fences are bowed outward toward the road.

"Look how silly those cows are," he says. "They lean against the fences, not realizing they could break through, fall onto the road, and be killed. They want to walk up the road and find other fields when they have their own green pastures they can romp through."

More fences pass by.

"I read somewhere that a cow's brain is the size of a human fist," I add helpfully. "Those cows sure are dumb...."

We ride a little while longer when my dad shifts in his seat and says, "Beth, you are like the cow, and I am like the fence. The Lord has provided you with so many green pastures to find satisfaction in, and I feel like all you do is press against the fence. Don't you realize if you break through, there's danger on the other side?"

He spends the rest of our time talking about how rich his own pastures are for him. Listening to him talk about his relationship with Christ makes faith unbelievably attractive to me that day; it makes faith seem like a relationship, not an exercise. I learn how much we benefit when we stay away from the road. I learn that the benefit of the pasture is greater than the attraction of the road.

Maria loves the other side of the fence, the feeling that no one controls her. She loves the road more than the pasture. She has been on that road so long now that she strolls down the middle, not even dodging when she hears a car coming. To warn her about the dangers of that sort of life is pointless now, when what she needs to believe in is the peace and comfort and love offered back in the green pastures.

I still see Maria from time to time. She stops by my home to let me know where she is and how she's doing. She isn't ready to come off the road, but she has a gnawing curiosity about whether I still like it over here in the pasture.

Living my life on purpose — with joy and adventure, love and risk — is the best ministry plan I have. It's exactly what God had in mind when he said, "We are lamp stands on a hill." The apostle Peter tells us that we need to be ready at any time to give a reason for the hope we have.

I don't know when Maria will walk through my door, ready to leave the road, or if it will even be my door she walks through. But in the meantime, my goal is to make sure that she sees me enjoying the pastures whenever she sneaks a look.

Adriana manages to look beautiful, even when her outfits are dirty or don't match. She is smart, articulate, and a leader in many ways, and she is the perfect candidate to come to our campus and continue her studies. After years in a children's home, she spends a year with one family and then a few months with another and, through a series of events, comes to live in my home one August. At sixteen, she is on the honor roll and the captain of her soccer team. We have no reason to expect less than a very bright future for her.

One night that fall, I'm at a dinner party with Adriana and a boy she's in love with. But the problem is, he isn't in love with her. It's a common dilemma, but when the monster in your closet is named "abandonment," it can make ordinary sadness grow into a distracting and destructive pain. That is the last night I remember Adriana feeling normal.

"He — " She starts to speak but stops.

I wait while she catches her breath.

"He ... he ... said he had another girlfriend, and-that-it-wasn't-about-me," she says in one breath. "But I just want to go home now. Can we leave?"

We ride in silence the whole way home. I bite my tongue. *She doesn't want my insights now*, I think.

That night, Adriana finds some comfort in eating ice cream out of the tub and watching a movie called *A Walk to Remember*, a love story about a terminally ill young girl whose boyfriend marries her so she can have a wedding. It's a familiar scene for any teenage girl trying to anesthetize the pain of loneliness. When we go to bed that night, she seems sad, but I assure her every woman has experienced a night like this and hers too will pass.

Later that night, I remember being shaken. "Beth, wake up —" I can just make out Adriana's face in the darkness. "Beth, I don't feel well. I think I'm getting sick."

"If you were in bed, you wouldn't be getting anything but sleep right now." I'm awake enough to feel grumpy. "I'm sure it's all that ice cream. Just go back to bed, and we'll talk about it in the morning." I hug her goodnight and walk her back to bed. Kissing her forehead, I say a quick prayer.

She wakes up feeling well enough to go to school but comes home talking really strangely. "I think I may be dying," she says.

"You're not dying; everyone in the planet has experienced what you did yesterday. You'll be just fine," I say. "There will be another boy."

"No, really. I think I'm sick. Pay attention to me. What would you do if I really was dying?" She insists, and I think to myself that she's awfully testy.

I pause and answer, "I'd be sad we didn't have more time together."

"I don't think you'd be the only one," she answers vaguely and goes to her room.

Over the next two days the situation worsens. Her delusions become more extreme. She tells her classmates she's terminally ill, and one of them even starts a fund to collect money for her treatment. She begins to lie about other things, and that night she doesn't sleep at all.

By the fourth day, we're on high alert. We call the hospital and ask the operator for the psychiatric ward.

"Before we can admit her," the psychiatrist explains, "she has to be a danger to herself or others."

"So there is nothing we can do?" I plead. "She's losing touch with reality."

"Honestly, you just have to wait till she becomes self-destructive. When the scale tips and you feel threatened, that's when you need to bring her in. If you bring her in too early, it'll just make her angry and might cause her to turn against you when she returns home. If you're too late, she could hurt someone. So stay vigilant."

Vigilant? Try hyper-alert. We sleep behind locked doors and stop trying to "talk sense" into her. She even rejects our prayers.

Six days later, Adriana's emotional and mental downward spiral spin to a climactic end. Todd and our friends Gabriel and Matt whisk her away in the car, bound for the emergency room at the hospital where she'll later be admitted to the psychiatric ward. As they pull out of the driveway, I look around at my house and at my other children and move around, cleaning up in shock. I am full of the emotions I've held in all week and devastated for Adriana's lost future. I feel for the children who have watched it all unfold and don't understand. I want to cry for her siblings who are afraid, and I cry for Adriana, knowing that she will be restrained and drugged and who knows what else in the days that follow.

Later we discover that Adriana's father probably also suffered from severe schizophrenia, though their family describes him as "bewitched."

"Who are you here to see?" the bored receptionist asks when we go to the hospital to visit Adriana for the first time.

"Adriana," I reply simply.

"Oh, you mean *Selena*. Today she's claiming she's a famous singer," the receptionist laughs. It is a mocking laugh that sounds evil.

My friend and I look at each other, and I think of the healthy Adriana we knew just a few days before. What happened?

We wind our way through the facility, which is dark and cramped. *Where are you, Lord?* I wonder, feeling drained. We reach the door that opens to an inner courtyard, and there Adriana is waiting, having been told she has visitors.

I gasp. She looks poised, beautiful in her government-issued grey hospital gown. She seems put together, calm. My mind runs through all of God's promises for orphans: that he will not leave her, he will maintain her cause, he will incline his holy ear, he will provide for her, he will be her Father ...

In this place, where she will stay for many months to come, there is so much darkness that it's almost suffocating. But, as though in beams of virtual light, she basks in the presence of the One who has had her in his sight since she was formed and can see her whole in eternity. I don't know why this had to happen to her.

Although she still has many dark days to walk through, with many medicines that will need adjustment and people who will treat her as a problem. This I know: during that visit and the subsequent ones, I saw that God had deposited a special grace in that girl and it won't go away whether she is in an orphanage, my home, or a psychiatric ward. She's still his creation, his child, and anyone who looks at her can see his stamp.

Still, the aftermath of Adriana's breakdown is a dark place — and not just for her. Her siblings are afraid of getting what she has. She exposed the most private secrets of many children while she was in our home and not in her right mind. The sponsors of her education were frustrated and confused because we hadn't foreseen this. Her roommate was traumatized by watching her close friend literally transform before her eyes.

Maria and Adriana.

Two women who live under the same sky I do — whose lives are worth fighting for. Where are the happy endings? I don't know. I want them so badly.

Still, my hope comes from wondering, Could it be that the intersection of their lives and mine is just one finite point in an eternal existence, that at this point in time I simply cannot judge how their lives will ultimately turn out?

Is my faith reckless enough to trust first and think second? Can I grow faith strong enough (like a muscle) that when it has to pick up a heavy reality, I can easily lift it and still have hope? That doesn't mean I don't think about consequences and pain, but I layer those on top of faith instead of the other way around. When we try to lay our faith on top, all the doubts and questions on the bottom make for an unstable foundation, and it almost always cracks. But when we have faith at the base, the questions, when they come, don't insist on being answered right away.

Some Christians, in the name of authenticity, wave their unanswered questions like flags of honor. They prefer to "be real" rather than believe easy answers or obey rules they don't totally embrace. And while I do think an authentic faith is clearly the better choice, sometimes it's just lazy to not try and push ourselves a little farther on in the faith journey.

> *Job answered God: "I'm convinced: You can do anything and everything. Nothing and no one can upset your plans. You asked, 'Who is this muddying the water, ignorantly confusing the issue, second-guessing my purposes?' I admit it. I was the one. I babbled on about things far beyond me, made small talk about wonders way over my head. You told me, 'Listen, and let me do the talking. Let me ask the questions. You give the answers.' I admit I once lived by rumors of you; now I have it all firsthand—from my own eyes and ears! I'm sorry—forgive me. I'll never do that again, I promise! I'll never again live on crusts of hearsay, crumbs of rumor."*
>
> Job 42:1 – 6 MSG

Reckless faith isn't fake. It doesn't pretend. It feels deeply and lives fully. It asks questions and cries out and tests boundaries. It has dynamic conversations with God. It molds its understanding as it encounters new situations and experiences new growth. "God has a plan" is not a cliché or Band-aid you put on wounds that aren't healing.

"God has a plan" is a mantra for a way of life that says you don't have to have all the answers to proceed. You can throw yourself toward the Red Sea and believe if it parts, praise God! You knew it!

How does it open? Why does it open now when it didn't earlier? Why did it close on the Egyptians? To those questions, you apply a faith that acts first and thinks second. Not in mindless obedience, but with childlike faith.

> *"I know what I'm doing. I have it all planned out — plans to take care of you, not abandon you, plans to give you the future you hope for. When you call on me, when you come and pray to me, I'll listen. When you come looking for me, you'll find me. I'll make sure you won't be disappointed." God's Decree. "I'll turn things around for you … bring you home to the place from which I sent you off into exile. You can count on it."*

Jeremiah 29:11 – 14 MSG

God promises us that our disappointments will not last forever. He turns things around, he brings us back, he takes us home. He rebuilds, restores, repairs.

It is still in my nature, on occasion, to push against the fence. I can lean and lean and return to the same questions or same sin or same fear, and it results in breaking through to the road. There I am subject to the consequences of the sin I have just committed.

But now there is a difference. Now I strive for a reckless faith, a faith that promises me that God forgives me and has a plan, and that plan is the best. His plan is for eternity, and his purposes don't need to be revealed in the short term just so I feel better now. So I dust off my bum wherever I've fallen, I pick up my pride, I unpack my questions, and I walk back over to the green pastures, where I find relief and joy untold. I then yell to all the other dumb cows that followed me or watched me curiously, and I tell them it wasn't worth it.

ELEVEN

Refugees

"Why are some of them naked?"

It's an innocent question. I'm sixteen years old, on my first missions trip, and we have just arrived at a refugee camp on the border between Costa Rica and Nicaragua.

One of the hosts says, "Well, they've just walked over eighty miles through the wilderness. Most of them have used their clothes to burn, bury the dead, trap animals, eat—"

Another volunteer impatiently asks, "Why? Does it bother you?"

Yes, it did, but I'm not offended by their nudity. Rather, I'm saddened and moved by it.

I spend that day alternating between dispersing used clothing and performing a drama our team has prepared—all of which creates a wave of conflicting feelings in me. I wonder whether the clothing or the drama matter more to God. In the back of my mind, I picture my own amply filled closet, and I feel confused.

On our last day at the camp, I don't want to leave. I need to know how I can keep helping, even after our group has left. So I march up to the busy director and ask him breathlessly, "Tomorrow I'm leaving, but tell me what can I do today?"

"We need clothes and food. It's pretty simple." And he walks away.

I think now I would recognize this as a brush off, but I left feeling commissioned.

"We are gathering clothes for needy Nicaraguans ..."

That fall, with my prepared slide show, flyers, and thoughts, I go to area high schools, promising if they give up their used clothing, we will deliver it to those who need it most.

I then arrange with a local amusement park to use their passenger pick-up area one fall afternoon, where I stand and wait as people come by to drop off their boxes.

"Dad, look at all these boxes!" I practically squeal with excitement later that day.

My father has taken off work to be there with me. The boxes have started to accumulate when a man pulls up to unload his bags from the trunk of his Monte Carlo.

"Hey," he says, pulling out his wallet, "are you taking cash donations for the shipping?"

I just stand there, stunned. *Shipping?* I'd never thought of *that* detail. In all my weeks of planning, it never occurred to me that I'd need to *pay* to have all these clothes shipped.

The man looks at me, waiting for a response, and I have none. After all the promises I've made, I stand there and wonder if I can really keep them.

My dad comes up behind me and says to the man, "There's been a private donation given to cover the shipping expenses." Satisfied, the man shrugs, puts his five dollars back in his pocket, and drives off.

I turn around and look at my dad. Without even asking I know that he and my mom are the ones making this "private donation."

The journey I am on today started back then, on the day I delivered those packages in several trips to the postal service.

At sixteen, I wasn't thinking strategically. Maybe that's why Jesus told us to have a childlike faith. Not until years later did it occur to me how ridiculous it was to write such a large check to a shipping company to send old

This is my dad with me at my wedding in 1994.

shoes to Latin America. It would have been wiser to write that same check to an organization in that country, where it could have purchased three times the amount of used clothing onsite.

But, of course, that's not the point. That day my dad was following the prompting of the Holy Spirit in his heart, and he obeyed. The Holy Spirit saw my whole life and knew that this event was the beginning of a much larger adventure.

So often our economy and God's are not the same. Though it might not have made sense to my dad to spend his money that way, following God's will doesn't always look logical. It can sometimes look downright reckless. You see, my dad wasn't just paying to ship old clothes overseas; his check was really seed money for something that took root in my heart. Now, whenever I find myself only making decisions based on "what makes sense," I stop and ask the Lord if I'm missing something. Is there another decision that involves something I don't necessarily understand but should be willing to obey?

The year before I moved to Mexico and the "missionary" events of my life began to unfold, my dad died of cancer. On this side of eternity he may have wondered whether his contribution to my clothing fund was really a smart decision, but from his perspective now, as a member of that great cloud of witnesses, he knows that such investments, directed by the Lord, pay off in ways not humanly conceivable.

How easy it is for me to make my faith look "refined." Under the guise of good stewardship, I can plan and plot my way toward responsible living. I'm a mother, and I have a savings account; I have insurance, and most days I drive the speed limit. I take vitamins and don't carry credit card debt. Responsible living is a good thing, but does it always need to look so refined? Can't we throw caution to the wind from time to time — and spend money on a used clothing project — not because it makes sense but simply because God asks us to?

A refined faith has charts and programs and plans. It's full of calculated steps and hand wringing. A refined faith is impressed with the big deals, big buildings, and big numbers. Certainly, God sometimes orchestrates big deals and provides for big buildings — but he is not counting heads. He just counts the hairs on *each* head.

A reckless faith, by contrast, understands that the best use for an expensive bottle of perfume may be to wash someone's feet. A reckless faith builds an ark before there's even a cloud in the sky. A reckless faith charges into the sea before thinking that God may part the water. A reckless faith leaves ninety-nine sheep to go after one lost one. It does not need man's approval — or man's money. It honors God in the classroom, even when no one else there reveres him. A reckless faith doesn't make moral compromises at the office, even when they're expected. A reckless faith believes in "till death do us part."

Unrefined does not mean immature or unthinking. The truth is, the closer I grow to God, the more experiences and knowledge I accumulate, the more recklessly I desire to live.

As a result, I want to ask God to heal my friend without mumbling that even if he doesn't, I'll try again later. I want to give away more than 10 percent, since I know how to live comfortably with whatever is left over. I want to say yes to projects and relationships even when they sometimes don't make sense.

I was commissioned that day on the border of Nicaragua and Costa Rica — but now I know that my commission had nothing to do with clothes. My commission is to have an "unstrategic," almost childlike faith, so I can respond to holy nudges.

A sweet smile!

TWELVE

José Angel

It is March and it's beautiful outside. We're spending the weekend traveling to Texas and enjoying some family fellowship and Texas hospitality. It should have been the perfect weekend, but as I walk along San Antonio's famed Riverwalk, all I can think about is where is the closest bathroom. I've been battling a stomach flu for a week now, and I'm getting tired of it.

A month later, while at the Easter service at church, I have to leave in the middle because my stomach is upset again. "How long has this been going on now?" I wonder.

May and June are a blur. We eventually ask the doctors why I can't keep food down anymore. I've never been sick as an adult; I have never even had allergies. So this new situation is both frustrating and irritating to say the least.

By July, the doctors have a diagnosis: gastroparesis, a condition in which your food doesn't digest, so after an extended time in your stomach, it has to come back up. The only problem is, there's no reason for me to have developed this condition. Most people who have it are diabetic, have had intestinal surgery, or have some sort of tumor or blockage.

Also, the doctors add, this condition usually gets progressively worse and has no cure.

On the last day of July, José Angel, a pastor friend of ours, comes to our house. Although he has a limited education, is missing a couple of teeth, and has an appearance like he forgot to get ready that morning, he has a heart of pure gold.

I have trouble admitting weakness. I don't like to ask people for help. The real name for it is *pride*.

Pastor José Angel is not one of my most intimate friends, so I haven't told him about the extent of my illness. All he knows is that I haven't been coming around the squatter village, where he has his ministry, as much as I used to — which makes his following comment to me even more amazing.

"Beth, I had a dream last week, and I'm sorry it has taken this long to get over here and tell you about it. There's no excuse. I know you've been sick, but I want you to know that God has healed you."

At that moment my conservative roots kick in, and I lift an eyebrow in skepticism.

José Angel continues, "In my dream there was a demon wrapped around your stomach, but it has now been released. God has allowed it for a season so when you encounter demonic forces in the future, you'll recognize them and how they move. He wants to use you to free others. But today *you* are free, so go, and walk in your

Pastor José Angel, his wife, Delores, and me

healing." He finishes and smiles.

Never before have I heard or experienced anything like that. Not one thing in his entire story seems believable to me. Still, I let him pray over me, but I feel no "tingling" of miraculous healing. So I walk back to the house, get sick, and feel frustrated.

Late one night two days later, my friend Sonia, who's married to another pastor here in Mexico, calls me on the phone. She sounds anxious: "*Oye*, Beth, I just had this dream about you and *had* to call and tell you about it ..." and she proceeds to describe the same dream that Pastor José Angel had — same message, same promise of healing.

The odd thing is that Pastor José Angel and Sonia don't even know each other. Now God has my attention.

I have scheduled a trip home to Ohio the next week, and while there I plan to see a medical specialist to pursue further treatment. I wrestle with what to tell him. I'm not even sure what to think myself.

In his office, I say, "Here's my file, here's my tests, here's my health history — and here's my frustration with the last couple of months." I probably tell him far more than he needs to know.

He nods, says "hmmm" a few times, looks over the files, and shutting the folder, concludes, "You're a very sick girl."

I look away for a moment. Should I tell him about the dreams? Oh, why not! I think. So I dive in. "You see, here's the thing, for the past week, I *have* been feeling better. Not all-at-once better or anything, but a little better every day. I've been eating some, and it's been staying down. I don't know how you feel about this — I don't really know how *I* feel about it — but I think a demon may have been released, and I have been healed."

"Wow." He pauses to collect his thoughts. "Normally, since these tests are less than a month old, I would use them to determine my treatment plan, but in light of your new testimony, let's repeat them and see where we stand."

That seems logical and safe. I like what I can read on a chart. So I drive to Good Samaritan Hospital the next day and repeat the myriad of tests.

Days later, the specialist calls me. "Beth, in my left hand are the test results you brought from Mexico that showed me you are a very sick girl. But in my right hand are the tests you took yesterday that tell me you are a hundred percent healthy. I don't know about those dreams your friends had, but I propose no ongoing medical treatment for you at this time." He pauses, then adds, "And yes, I do think it's a miracle."

I don't understand it, but I need to testify to it. Do I think that a demon had his "hand" around my stomach? I don't know, but it sure felt like it. If faith could fit in a frame, the way a painting does, then we might get tired of looking at it after a couple of years. But faith, as it grows, keeps demanding a new and larger frame to be housed in. I think the Lord loves to do things that are unexpected, things that are beyond what we can control or predict. It forces our canvas to get bigger. These days I just try to expand first and wait till later to figure it all out.

Ultimately, God moves me. He consistently breaks the boundaries (my frame) with which I've surrounded him. It means admitting my finiteness and rigidity. It means he is dangerously greater than I can define or even understand. I am different now: I minister differently, I pray differently, I look for new aspects of his character. Never say "never." That has been the lesson of this past year. I now drive a minivan, have given my toddler Diet Coke, and have had an up-close-and-personal encounter with a demon.

Some people would look at José Angel, with his ragged appearance and lack of education, and think about all the ways they could "teach and train" him. But I'm not sure I can ever match what he offered to me that July afternoon. He was listening to the Lord so intently that he caught a message meant for me. Then he trusted in the Spirit that led him to my door to share what must have been uncomfortable.

There is no way to teach or train someone to have that kind of faith. Pastor José Angel's is a humble, quiet sort of faith — a faith which is unbelievably *reckless*.

THIRTEEN

Rodolfo

The first time I meet Rodolfo, I am doling out backpacks at the children's home where he lives. I'm trying to make sure every child receives one — and only one. Some of the boys have gotten back in line, taking advantage of the fact that I'm distracted and haven't yet learned all their names. By the time Rodolfo approaches me, I realize that some boys have two or even three backpacks strapped on their backs. My good humor vanishes.

"May I have two?" he asks. He is about eleven years old but speaks like an adult. The way he asks me, however, makes me want to say yes.

"No, you can't. I only have enough for each child to have one," I answer, wondering why he has put his hand on a pink one.

"Okay," he concedes, letting go. "My little sister is sick today and couldn't get in line. I want to make sure she gets one." He hands me the Tinkerbell bag that he has just been looking at. "Could you deliver this to her dorm for me? Her name is Ruth," he says.

I'm stunned by his sensitivity. I take the backpack and watch him walk away — without a backpack for himself. He is now on my radar.

The next day I look for him and find him studying for exams. Most sixth graders don't take exams seriously, especially in a place where no one is impressed by good grades. But he is bent over his books for most of the afternoon. I bring him a Coke and rub his back for a moment, before leaving him alone. There is something different about Rodolfo.

Later that spring, at his sixth grade graduation, I watch him accept the academic first-place prize. I whoop and holler like I'm at a rodeo, and he flashes me a quiet smile.

Over the next three years, as Rodolfo makes his way through junior high, I study him. I learn about his life at the orphanage and who his friends are. Todd and I invite him over to our house for dinner and out for an occasional pizza, since Rodolfo has become fascinated with English and practices with anyone who will help him build his vocabulary.

Rodolfo is the oldest of three siblings — who live in the children's home. His unmarried mother has never been in a position to care for them. Whenever children have a family member — a grandmother, husband, aunt, uncle — to take care of the mother, they can usually be cared for as well, but if no one is around to support the mother, in most cases she can't keep the family together. Every day Todd and I try to help those suffering from the collateral damage of broken families and poverty — and Rodolfo grew up a victim of both.

In the months leading up to graduation from junior high school (ninth grade is the end of mandatory education in Mexico), we begin to speak to him about his future. "You're once again graduating first in your class," we tell him. "You have all the potential in the world to do or be whatever you want …" We preach the same message in various forms over and over. *Lord, help him hear what he cannot yet see.*

On the night of Rodolfo's ninth-grade graduation, rain is pouring down outside. We've planned a party for him at our home afterward, and I've decorated the house in the colors of the high school he has agreed to attend. We are thrilled that he is willing to take the next step but we are also aware of his anxiety and fears.

"That was a great ceremony. You have so much to be proud of! I can't believe it …" I'm almost babbling in the car on the way home. "What you said was great. I took tons of pictures. Did you hear us screaming when they called your name?"

The more I filled the air with my comments, the quieter he got.

"Rodo, what's wrong?" I finally ask.

"My mom was there, Beth. She wants me to come home. To work … so I can support the family. It might mean my siblings could come home too. There are lots of factories near her home." He looks at us, painfully conflicted.

Rodolfo with staff friend, Jim Betscher

We are quiet for the rest of the ride home. Todd turns off the car, and we listen to the rain falling hard on the car roof.

"Rodolfo," Todd begins, "you are smart enough to make your own life decisions, and ultimately you are the one who has to live with them. But what you have lacked all these years is someone who was looking out for *your* best interests. I want to be that person. I know you have waited a long time to 'go home,' so why don't you go there this summer and think long and hard about how you want the rest of your life to unfold."

That was all he said. We hug Rodolfo, go in to the party, celebrate with the valedictorian, and then say goodbye to him for the summer.

When fall rolls around, the week that school starts, there's a knock at our door. I open the door, and there stands Rodolfo. He doesn't say a thing (words are so overrated sometimes), but it's clear that he has come to our house because he's decided to continue his studies. Neither of us is sure what to say, so we just hug. I invite him in, and we play with my children and watch TV for the afternoon until Todd comes home.

At this point we have nowhere for Rodo to live, no boys' home program, no extra space. We have twin girls living under our roof, so we know that he can't stay with us. After experiencing sweet sixteen-year-old freedom all summer, he voluntarily checks himself back into the orphanage so he can go to high school.

A few days later, when Todd drives him to his new school, Rodolfo looks at Todd, looks out the window at his school, looks back at Todd again, and says, "I'm not going in."

Todd gives him a questioning look.

"I'm leaving," says Rodolfo. "I'm sorry. I thought this was what I wanted, but I was wrong. I can't do it." He sure *looks* ready — new shoes, new backpack, a scientific calculator — but he can't cover up what is screaming at him from inside.

They pray, and Todd shoves him out the door. "One day, Rodo. Just give it today and see how you feel. I'll come and pick you up after school, and we can talk more then." And then he speeds off before Rodo can object.

Rodolfo survives that day and decides to return. He has to work harder than all the other students who have gone to better junior highs, have played on computers for years, and have taken more classes in English. But he succeeds. Rodolfo learns those skills and becomes hungry for more. He balances all of that with his responsibilities at the children's home and his homework until we open our boys' home, and he moves onto our campus the following year.

Before we know it, we are sitting at his high school graduation and celebrating his achievements. Not only is he first in his class once again, but he has been accepted at an engineering school with a great scholarship. He has a wonderful future ahead of him.

"We couldn't be more proud, Rodolfo!" we tell him. "You'll be a great engineer."

That fall he enters college with blossoming confidence. But then, it happens.

"Beth, Todd, I *hate* school," he tells us one late fall afternoon as he sits on our couch. "I hate school. I don't want to be an engineer. Whose idea was *that* anyway? Was that mine? If so, I don't know what I was thinking." He shakes his head. "I have a dream. I love languages. My dream is to speak lots of languages."

"And do what, actually, as a job?" my practical husband quizzes.

"I don't know. I can't do engineering for four years, let alone the rest of my life. I'm not afraid of hard work. It's not that the classes are too hard. It's just that I have no *heart* for it."

We listen to him and decide together that he should follow his heart. The next day he enrolls in an undergraduate linguistics program where he studies five languages — simultaneously. Soon he is graduating with his bachelor's degree, once again first in his class.

Life has never been easy for Rodolfo, but he has learned to use his difficult circumstances to strengthen, not weaken, himself.

One day a little while later, while I'm helping him pull his résumé together, I say, "You are much more than the sum of what's written on this paper. You are a journey. You have walked places many of us can't imagine, and you have done it with excellence. You have refused to allow your circumstances to define you. You're stunning!"

He rolls his eyes at me, knowing I'm just warming up.

"Really," I say, "most people would have sat down and given up at a hundred points in your journey, but you chose to stand back up and keep walking. I've always known that your decisions all the way along would benefit you greatly someday, but now I realize that those decisions are going to benefit your siblings and your mother as well — and those decisions will have a huge impact on whoever you marry and on your children and grandchildren. Do you know how much hope you offer to those who are growing up in your children's home and to all the people who meet you and are inspired by your journey?"

He looks away, thoroughly embarrassed.

"God chose you," I say. "He empowered you. He's using you. He filled you up. He gave you courage, strength, understanding, patience. There's no way he will give up now. He built you and built those qualities into you, and the light you shine is blinding!"

How did Rodolfo travel from the painful point of drop-off to this lighthouse of inspiration? The distance between the two is far enough, and not many are willing to make the journey. How does God build any of us up into who we are today? He does so patiently, bringing people and circumstances into our lives, and he even uses, for his good, what the Enemy intends for our harm. God is our ultimate cheerleader, calling out to us to look beyond what life hits us with and see him who is creating us and forming us and making us more like himself.

What I see in Rodolfo is the good God is doing in him. God made him strong, God made him smart, God made him who he is, and God waits at every turn to help Rodolfo (and all of us) discover that. No orphanage, no worker, no snotty-nosed high school girl, no future employer — no one can take away from Rodolfo what God has built in him. What God builds always lasts.

The children we meet in the children's homes go through the classic stages of grief: first they experience *shock* ("Are you kidding me? Why is this happening to me? What do you mean I can't get out?"). Then they experience *denial/ isolation* ("My mother will come back — just as soon as she cleans up her addiction, marries her boyfriend, changes jobs

…"). As the denial subsides, it is replaced with *anger* ("I hate her! I hate you! I hate God! I hate school!"). Anger costs too much energy, and so slowly they settle into something quieter, *depression* ("Why me? What's wrong with me?"). Then, those who look at what's in front of them and decide to step up on the block, instead of stumbling over it, have *acceptance/resolution* ("This is who I am, but I am not defined by where I am").

The children who make it through to the last stage are the ones that come out with a stronger inner core, a character that no one can touch. The ones who stay mired in the grief process end up as part of the statistical 90 percent of orphans worldwide who go into the black market or prostitution. They still feel defined by circumstances they had no control in shaping.

For me, Rodolfo's life will always be a signpost that signifies a certain kind of reckless faith. It reads: We are yet to be all God has created us to be, and the effort it takes to move forward is worth it!

FOURTEEN

Dialogue in the Darkness

The sign outside the building reads: Dialogue in the Darkness. A girlfriend of mine and I joke that it must be a marriage counseling center. But it isn't. We are on a school field trip to a workshop on understanding people with disabilities. For an entire hour during the course of this workshop, both children and adults will be guided through a completely darkened building, making our way through various common circumstances that people with vision challenges face in everyday life.

The facilitator tells us, "The most important rule is to listen for your guide. She will walk with you through the course, and she knows the path ahead. When she tells you to stop, stop! When she tells you to watch for the upcoming traffic, bridge, or other obstacle, take note."

Beto, eyes wide open, is a boy on our campus, learning to live according to the voice of his Guide

Then we break into small groups, and my team receives its red-tipped canes.

As we head into the large building, which is completely dark inside, one of the kids begins to cry and is escorted back to the light.

"What do you feel?" says our guide.

I think she means something different, but I can't help calling out, "Lost."

She leads us through many common locales, including a grocery store, a "wooded" area with trees and unstable footing, a boat, and a restaurant.

Most of the children are quiet, focusing in on their next step. The only saving grace is the voice of the guide. She seems to be able to anticipate our moves before we do!

She knows when to be encouraging and when to sternly direct our steps across a street. Sometimes the other sounds threaten to drown out her voice, but she can always be heard if you strain or call out. Okay, okay, okay … I get it, Lord; I will listen better for your voice, I dialogue inside my head.

Finally, an hour later, at the end of our experience and exhausted from the concentration it requires, we sit down with our guide while still in the darkness to process how we feel. The children are full of comments:

"It was hard to not be able to just peek."

"I want to see the light."

"I was scared the whole time."

"I feel sorry for blind people."

I chip in, "I'm grateful that you could see ahead and tell us what to expect."

"Well, that's funny," said the guide. "You didn't realize that I'm actually blind — all the time, not just in here." Nobody says anything for a minute. Finally she adds, "I've just learned how to listen for clues."

Later that day, back in the world of light, I meditate on Isaiah 42:6 – 7:

> *I, the Lord, have called you in righteousness; I will take hold of your hand. I will keep you and will make you to be a covenant for the people and a light for the Gentiles, to open eyes that are blind, to free captives from prison and to release from the dungeon those who sit in darkness.*

When Jesus called the disciples, they dropped their nets — their entire lives — and followed him. When he calls us, we don't do much net dropping any more, and sometimes we feel that we can just keep doing what we've always been doing — only better with God at our side. But Jesus said, "Deny yourself, pick up the cross and *follow* me." To follow the voice of the Guide is to let go of our own agenda and throw ourselves towards his. How much more reckless can you get than that?

Puri and Esteban

Singing in worship this morning, I came to the line, "When there is pain in the offering ... blessed be your name." I wondered, Are we really asked to invite pain into our offerings — or does it only refer to the pain that comes and finds us?

It's so hard to undo the message, constantly reinforced in our culture, that says we deserve happiness and recognition and special treatment. What do we really deserve? Comfortable shoes? A peaceful retirement? Parents? Or is anything of value that I have or receive a literal gift?

Which is harder to offer up, a painful offering or a comfortable one? Most days when I am experiencing pain, I am willing to let it go (to offer it, in other words), and I want to see God use it, to make sense of it. But it's my creature comforts that I find hard to throw into the offering.

"*Es Mío!*" He tugs at the car.

"*No, Mío!!*" The other tugs back harder.

"*MÍO!*" That scream rises above the constant din and finally gets my attention.

You don't have to understand Spanish to get the picture.

Two brothers.

One remote control car.

One holds the control, the other the car. And at the top of their lungs, each is screaming his own claim over this new toy.

At first, I try to reason with them, though it is hard to follow my logic over the noise of their ruckus. Then I resort to threats. It makes me feel temporarily powerful, but ultimately it's ineffective. Then I act uninterested — but the fight continues.

Finally I say to the brothers, "What you can't share, you can't have," and I take the car and the remote and walk away.

Minutes later, they approach me, all their energy now focused like a laser beam on me. "We will share it; we want to have it back," they plead.

I relent. I really do want them to have it after all. Someone sent it to the orphanage and these boys are perfect candidates to enjoy it. I had no pleasure in being the one who took it away. An hour later, they are still taking turns driving their car around the basketball court, and I smile.

A little ray of light ...

Sometimes I wish God would snatch things away from me when I'm not sharing. It would help me learn my lesson more quickly. But then, when he does take things away, I can make quite a ruckus myself.

What we cannot share, we cannot keep for long. What we share ends up multiplying and returning to us more than its original promise. The boys looked at that car and saw fun, but what they gained by sharing it was not only fun, but cooperation and friendship as well. I watched them that day on the court and wondered what blessings I have robbed myself of simply because I wouldn't share.

"Beth, you won't believe what happened this weekend."

I am eating breakfast when one of our Mexican staff comes in to tell me about her Sunday lunch. She continues, "I went with my family to the chicken stand, and we were all sitting there eating our tortillas and chicken, when I felt the Holy Spirit prompt me to talk to a woman who was there with her large family. I wish I could say that I went right over, but I didn't, and all the way home I was chiding myself for not following through. Once I got home, the Spirit would not let me rest, so I explain to my husband we have to go back in case she's still there. And you know what? She *was* still there.

So I walk up and just tell her the Lord has directed me to her, and I ask if there is anything she would like me to pray for. She laughs and tells me that she and her husband have a small orphanage and that she imagines the Lord already knows all the needs she has, but she would appreciate the encouragement anyway.

"Can you believe that?" she finishes. "I told her that's what we do. We need to go and visit their home. We just have to." She looks at me in a way that makes *me* feel it's urgent. "I have to believe we were supposed to meet."

We make a date to go to see their home, and my first impression is that it's incredibly small. I notice the walls don't reach the roof, there aren't enough beds, the refrigerator's empty, and a myriad of other problems that signal the extreme poverty of those who live here. Lord, where do we start? I pray.

Just then a little girl walks up beside me and puts her arms up for a hug. I smile, knowing I was just sent the answer.

Puri, the woman whom my friend saw at the chicken stand, and her husband, Esteban, run this home. They have taken in a couple dozen children and live daily by God's manna. As the afternoon progresses, I have the privilege to hear more of their story; how God led them after a long season of infertility to their first baby girl, and then the next five, and now dozens; how in this home, called *Rayos de Luz* ("Rays of Light") the children feel grateful to be in a place where they are loved, safe, and fed every day.

Their situation demands a new level of understanding from me. The work they do and the conditions under which

Esteban, director of Rays of Light

they serve would break most of us in a week or so, and yet, they have cheerfully committed to a lifetime of service. They remind me of that song that says, "When there is pain in the offering, blessed be your name."

We invite Puri, Esteban, and their children over to our home to swim while we have a group visiting from the U.S. We ask the team to clean up what they were working on so they can get ready for the kids coming over.

One of the visiting women thinks to herself, *Why can't we just keep working? The last thing I want to do is get into my bathing suit to play with kids all day.* She walks into the building and wonders if anyone will notice if she just stays in bed all afternoon.

Across town, one of the kids from Rayos de Luz is thinking, *I'm not leaving again.* He shivers with fear, as the other kids pile into the van. *I didn't do anything to anyone and no one has even talked to me yet. What could I have done wrong already?* He's confused, but refuses to ask anyone.

As their van makes its way down the highway toward our home, this elementary aged boy is thinking over his last forty-eight hours. He finally admitted to the director of his previous orphanage that someone was hurting him to the point of terror. He hoped for protection, a refuge, but instead he was picked up a couple of hours later by a stranger and had to face a new kind of terror: a new children's home, new kids, new school … He has only been at Puri and Esteban's place since yesterday, but already he hears the same line: "We're going to go and meet some new kids and have fun this afternoon." *Yeah*, the boy thinks to himself, *I've heard that before ... I will not get out this time. I won't be tricked again.*

When the van reaches our place and pulls through the gate, he sees other kids already running around a green lawn. *I won't talk to anyone*, he thinks. *I won't look at anyone, and maybe no one will notice me. I won't let them leave me here.*

When our visiting missionary worker from the U.S. hears someone shouting, "Everyone come on out! The kids are here!" she decides it's too lazy to stay in bed all afternoon, so she wanders down to the pool area, where she sees some Legos spread around on the ground. They remind her of how her son used to play with them, and she kneels

down to pick up some pieces. Out of the corner of her eye, she sees one young boy looking at her, desperately trying to look uninterested. She lifts a half-made Lego car to him and motions for him to join her.

This is a trick, I know it, he thinks as he sees her gesture to him. He quickly looks away.

He'd probably rather swim than play with an old lady like me anyway, thinks our visitor, as she moves her hand back quickly and goes back to picking up the pieces another child has knocked over.

What are those anyway? Is that a car she's making? He hates the fact that curiosity keeps him rooted to the spot.

Hey, he's looking this way again, she thinks. *I'll just move closer.* She smiles wryly at him and inches closer with her handful of Legos.

Then gently she raises her hand and offers them.

As he takes them, he looks into her eyes and offers her back a look of fear and hope combined. Those two emotions battle in him throughout the afternoon, but the pair never separate. She later admits to finding great comfort in his companionship and purpose for an afternoon she thought she was wasting.

He quietly acknowledges a friend, something he forgot how to enjoy.

I am impressed by the heroes of the faith. Amy Carmichael served orphans in India for decades without a furlough.

Corrie ten Boom ran her ministry until she died at an old age. Mother Theresa had an impact all over the world. The list is long and many names are not well known. Are these people superhuman servants who deserve to be up on a pedestal? Or did they simply learn along the way how to tap into what Puri and Esteban have discovered?

I took my niece to Rayos de Luz last week. Puri met us at the door with a little girl who had just arrived the day before. She wasn't quite two years old, and her eyes were full of fear. "Isn't she beautiful?" coos Puri. I agree with her that she is and then add that I bet she's keeping them up at night.

"Yes, she needs constant reassurance that we're still here" she answers, smiling.

I shake my head as I embrace her, wondering how she divides herself in so many pieces.

Then I remember something I heard in church once as a child. God is not part loving, part graceful, part peaceful, part forgiving. Instead he is all loving on top of all graceful on top of all peaceful. He is not divided up, so we each get a piece. We all get all of him we need, all the time.

My mind wanders to my home, where Todd and I are currently parenting nine children. How can I be more like God, instead of trying to break myself up in equal size pieces for everyone, which never feels good or works out right anyway? What if, instead, I could be all myself, wholly offered to him, so that he can spill out enough onto my family?

Is that how Puri does it? I wonder as I walk away. *Does she just look at God, and ask him to look at all twenty of them?*

When my sheets don't match or when the car needs work or when I am tempted to sit down and complain, I remember the little "rays of light" that live in abundance in places like Rayos de Luz. When there is pain in the offering, still, blessed be his name. More than any paycheck or possession, what God offers makes me rich, and his strength is more than enough for any work he has prepared in advance for me. I can let go of trying to make it all work, of creating my own kingdom. I can let go of escape routes and back-up plans. I can let go.

Sixteen

Evan

Long before I was ever married, I had in my heart a baby from another country.

On some of our early dates, Todd and I talked about adoption. When we were twenty-four, even though we had no infertility issues, we decided to act on those early plans. When, to our surprise and delight, I became pregnant with our daughter, Emma, we put all our adoption plans on hold. The agency we had worked with said we should wait until after the birth of our daughter and then resume if we were still interested. There was speculation among our extended family that "a baby of our own" would snuff out all our adoption talk — but it actually did just the opposite. Before, adoption had been only a desire, but now, a year later, when Emma was only a few weeks old, adoption had become a calling in our hearts.

On the weekend of July Fourth, 1998, we are driving north, reluctantly leaving Mexico for a job in the States. I feel disappointed to be leaving Mexico without an adopted baby, and Todd reminds me, "Honey, our lives aren't over yet."

"Yeah ... you're right, I'm sure," I mutter. I pick up Emma, look into her face and sing, "You have a brother or sister out there somewhere."

Emma and Evan, both walking, age two

A month later, I get an urgent call from the staff who replaced us in Monterrey. "Beth, I know you'd want to know this right away, but Ruth has been in an accident. She was hit by a car."

Ruth is a five-year-old girl I have grown to love in one of the orphanages. Apparently, she found herself on the wrong side of a car that came out of park on a hill. Within hours, I fly with a friend and three-month-old Emma to see how I can help our new staff facilitate Ruth's medical care. Days of hospital visits, medicines, and surgery follow.

When I finally have to head back home once again, I tell Ruth, "I'm leaving tomorrow." I stroke her forehead. "But they say you're going to be just fine." I slip her a piece of chocolate and feel overwhelmed with compassion for her.

That night, I stay in the house with the new staff, a house which had been ours until the month before. I'm packing my bags when the phone rings.

"Beth, will you get it?" shouts Terry from the other room. The phone is a hard place to practice my language skills.

"*Bueno*," I answer.

"Beth?"

"Yes?"

"It's Maria, I'm glad I found you. Sit down, Beth, I have a special story for you."

Maria tells me about a little baby boy, whom we later named Evan, abandoned and available for adoption. If Todd and I want to adopt him, we will need to travel the next day to Veracruz City and pick him up at noon. Veracruz is sixteen hours by car from Monterrey and a million miles, or so it seems, from Todd.

I sit down in the chair and put my head in my hands. Where am I? What am I doing? Emma interrupts my thoughts with her cries, and I pick her up. Is there a baby waiting somewhere for me at this very moment? Is he crying?

I hang up and kneel down next to the bunk bed in the guest room. I pray until my heart feels more settled (who am

I kidding?), and then pick up the phone again to call Todd. Moments of conversation end with him saying he'll meet me in Veracruz.

"You sure you can get off work?" I giggle uncontrollably. Nerves. "I mean, seeing as how you just started your new job a couple of hours ago?"

"Remember on the way home, when I told you that we will know when it's right? It's right."

What Satan intended for evil (the pain of a fatherless child), God used to demonstrate what he had planned since the beginning of time. In one motion he fulfilled his promise to Ruth ("to be a Father to the fatherless"), he fulfilled the longing of our hearts, and he fulfilled his commitment to Evan ("to place the lonely in families," Psalms 68:6).

The next day, as I fly to Veracruz, I am absolutely sure of what we are doing. I remember a ridiculous amount of detail from that day's journey: my taxi driver's name is José, and he wants to hold Emma. I fly in first class because it is the only seat left on the plane. I read the paper for the first time in Spanish, just to busy my mind. I meet Todd at an oceanside café called the Parador late that afternoon and order *two* desserts ...

When we check into the hotel and go to our room, I am in a frenzy. "Did they say they were going to pick us up in our room? Or were we supposed to be in the lobby?" I count diapers and choose *again* the clothes we are taking. "Did you drink my Diet Coke? Is it 4:00 our time? Or their time? What time is it here anyway? Did you change Emma?" Todd tries to reach out to hold me still, but I'm already gone from the place I was sitting and on the move again. It feels like labor, that crazy out-of-body experience where it's impossible to get comfortable. "Do you think this is enough formula? What if he needs that soy kind? Do they sell that here? Should I take a pacifier?" I am asking questions faster than Todd can answer them.

A knock comes on the door. I swing it open, thinking, okay, so they're going to pick us up at our room, and then my eyes land on him. I gasp.

"I was at the orphanage earlier today," says the attorney, even though I'm not really listening to him. I'm wholly focused on the baby in his arms. "And I thought I'd save you a trip and just bring him over. He hasn't eaten in a while, and his diaper

The Guckenbergers, August 2007

needs changing. Hope it's okay just to drop him by here like this. Enjoy your afternoon. I'll be by in the morning with the paperwork." With that, he hands our son to us and leaves.

I am immediately calm, and now it's Todd's turn to panic. I hold Evan, gaze at his beautiful brown eyes, sing to him, and cry a little. It is all so peaceful for me. But Todd is at the bathroom sink, yelling, "How do you make formula? I can't open this can!"

"Read the directions," I call out helpfully.

"They're in Spanish!" he retorts.

"You can read Spanish, honey," I sing back.

He begins a snappy comeback when we catch each other's eyes, and we dissolve into laughter.

"Where *are* we?" I ask him. It is so surreal.

"Together," he answers.

And we pray over our son for the first time.

By the next day, our antennas are up. Something's terribly wrong with our baby. His current weight is lower than his birth weight, and it's easy to see why. He struggles to eat, remains rigid in our arms, has trouble sleeping, and pants like he can't catch his breath. We keep reminding ourselves that God drew our family together, and there isn't anything he didn't know about in advance. Whatever the problem is, we'll solve it.

In Mexico adoptions take time, and soon Todd has to return to the States to work, and I stay behind with the babies. One day I get a call telling me to report to the American Embassy in Mexico City. I put Evan in one of those front carriers, and I leave Emma in the hotel with my sister-in-law, who has flown in to help.

"We are in the biggest city in the world, buddy," I whisper in Evan's ear while we cross a busy street on foot. "Let's hope they tell us you can go home today." I climb the steps and show my passport to the guard at the door. He ushers me into an office while I wait for the right person to appear with Evan's new paperwork. "Wanna see my baby?" I ask anyone who will listen. A couple of weeks have passed since we first set eyes on Evan, and despite the challenges his low weight and poor eating present, he feels more and more like my son every day.

Finally, an embassy official appears. Just by looking at him I can tell that horrible news is coming. "Mrs. Guckenberger, we've recently uncovered a baby smuggling ring, and as part of our investigation we're combing through the files of all the adoptions in the past three months. Since yours happened just two weeks ago, it's one of those under investigation."

"So what does that mean?" I am hoping to sound brave, maybe even defiant. But the way my voice breaks is a dead giveaway — I'm scared.

"We'll be going back to his hometown, interviewing the birth mother, doctors, anyone involved in any way with his adoption. He can remain in your custody, but it could take some time. If we find out that he was given or sold with coercion, then your adoption could be reversed."

I make no more attempts at bravery. I begin to cry — *hard*. No more "more and more like my son every day." A line has been drawn and now I am Mama Bear, and before me is a threat to my child. Something instinctual kicks in. Although I know that the man before me is just a messenger, I still feel the need to let him know exactly how I feel.

After my rampage, I walk out of the embassy, trembling.

In the days that follow, there are phone calls and threats, prayers and fasting. About ten days later we get a call: Evan's papers are ready and we can travel home.

Only seven weeks after Ruth was hit by the car, we are home, and a series of doctor visits begins for Evan. Keep in mind that adoption is not for the faint of heart, and the whole procedure leaves us a bit weary. I am delirious to begin with from sleep deprivation, and we are racking up travel, adoption, and medical expenses so fast it starts to feel like we are spending Monopoly money.

I am tired and distracted the afternoon we meet with Evan's neurologist. He tells me, "Your son will never walk."

I sit in the examination room, stunned. Evan plays on my lap with a toy keychain.

The neurologist continues, "Your son has profound cerebral palsy. The faster you accept him the way he is, the better it is for this child, who wants and needs to bond with you. So whatever you're thinking, whatever you thought when you adopted him, replace it now with the reality that you have a special-needs child."

On the way home, I let myself cry.

We already knew we loved this boy who was perfectly made and fit right with our family. That isn't what is being questioned. I was part brave, part unaware of the doctor's diagnosis and all the things he was saying: "He will never walk ... never live independently ..." Still, I recount in my head all the miracles I have seen God perform.

When I arrive home that afternoon, my tears have dried, but when Todd comes home from work, they start again as I recount the day's events.

We pray and then cry some more. We walk over to the nursery and see our two babies sleeping together. Emma is curled into a ball, relaxed and peaceful. Evan is crinkled along one side of his crib — his left hand sticks into the air at an awkward angle, as if it were a reminder of his condition.

A tremendous shift happens when a gnawing fear becomes confirmed. Hope temporarily dies, because it was a hope that what I fear isn't true. Then hope is reborn in the form of faith, faith that God will take over even if I can't yet see how.

Quickly we dive head first into the therapy circuit — occupational therapy, physical therapy, water therapy, sensory therapy. We have Emma and Evan spend as much time together as possible, which I soon learn is called "artificial twinning" and is in no professional's opinion a good idea. I keep saying, "It wasn't our idea either, but look how cute they are together." Still, I keep getting copies of journal articles and lectures on comparison. It doesn't help when

Emma begins to walk at seven months (having attended a few therapy sessions with her brother), and the head shaking and comparisons begin.

It hits me especially on the day I see Emma grab a Bob the Builder toy out of Evan's hand. She uses her mobility to her advantage, walking quickly across a room that takes Evan thirty minutes to crawl across.

Evan starts to cry, and I stop myself an instant before I'm about to scoop him up. The therapist's words echo in my head: "He won't solve his problems if you are always there to move him, Beth." She had told me earlier that same afternoon.

I just watch him struggle to climb up the chair so he can look Emma in the eye. Then he moves towards her, "cruising," they call it, as he uses his hands to steady himself on the couch, and focuses on his toy. When the couch ends and the toy is still out of reach, he steps forward, and I gasp, my eyes filling with tears. He takes another step. And another. And the tears now blur my view.

He's walking.

I scoop up Emma and Evan and we drive to show Todd at work. Todd doesn't make any jokes about our having a little linebacker or dancer in our future. Both of us are speechless, grateful, and humbled.

Todd breaks the emotion to laugh, "I know where you're headed next. Go on, but go easy on him."

I laugh. Soon I'm on the familiar route down the highway to Children's Hospital.

"Beth, you don't have an appointment today," the receptionist says when I walk into the office.

"Nope, I don't. But can I have a moment of the doctor's time?"

She sighs. I'm sure they must get interruptions like this all the time. She asks me if there is anything a nurse could address.

"I'd love for her to consult with me too, if she has a minute," I say.

When the doctor finally walks out into the reception area, my voice catches in my throat. I'm flustered and excited. I just set Evan down, and he walks over to the neurologist, a bit shaky, but on his own.

One step becomes a hundred more, and soon Evan is running. He is now a healthy, happy, soccer-playing boy who does advanced math and has no trace of cerebral palsy.

"What seems foolish to the world can be the wisdom of God," I begin my talk to a MOPS group one Tuesday morning. "I'm sure more than one person rolled their eyes as we came home with Evan. 'Can they handle it?' And more than once in the middle of the night, or during a grocery store meltdown, I was also asking the Lord, 'Can I handle it?'

"When I got married, we thought *we* were going to plan our family. I can safely tell you, this was never my plan. But it's much better."

In the end, most of Evan's doctors attribute his healing to his sister. I can tell you that *I* never planned to have two children seven weeks apart. Emma and Evan were God's plan. I can see, though, how God used Emma in Evan's life more than all the therapists and doctors combined. It was like being in therapy all day; chasing her, modeling her, mirroring her, communicating with her. Her example, companionship, and camaraderie drew Evan toward movements that we thought he would never master.

God is always God, even if he had not chosen to heal Evan. When I share Evan's story, I am constantly mindful of the families of special-needs babies. I do not pretend to understand why Evan was healed and others are not. But I do know what Jesus said about the blind man in John 9: "Neither this man nor his parents sinned, but this happened so that the works of God might be displayed in him."

"*No sé*," she says as she lets out the big breath she's been holding, "They told me to come here and talk to you, but I do not know where to start." The young girl came to my door minutes before I am headed out to the zoo with Emma and Evan. Todd and I are back now, living in Mexico and working in the orphanages. This girl looks young, vulnerable, and like she could benefit from a day at the zoo as well.

"I'm on my way out, but I'd love to talk." I glance down at her swollen abdomen. "Why don't you come with us, and we can talk about it while we are there?" I offer.

As we walk around that afternoon, she tells me she broke a glass Coke bottle earlier that week and swallowed the pieces, hoping to rid her body of a baby she had conceived during an unwanted sexual episode.

"Well, lesson number one," I say, "your reproductive organs and digestive tract are not interconnected."

Evan interrupts, pointing at the lions through the fence. "Lions! Stay here Mommy, please; I want to watch them."

The woman looks at me strangely. "He speaks English?"

"Yes," I explain, "he was adopted as a baby, so his first language is ours. I hope he'll learn Spanish one day, but for now it's Mommy, not *Mamá*."

The rest of the day she listens as I talk about her options for her unborn baby, but she later tells me it was all background noise. She couldn't stop watching and listening to Evan.

"Let's get together at the end of the week after you've had some time to think. Why don't we meet on Friday?" I am trying to create a moment where she has some accountability and closure. "Do you have any questions for me about what we talked about today?" We covered a lot, and I want her to fully understand so she can think clearly about her choices.

"Yes, I do have one." She looks down at my double stroller. "Do you love him? Like you do *her*?"

Stunned, I ask, "That's your question? Not about the medical things we discussed, or the spiritual, or the practical, or your care, or abortion, or adoption, or protection, or the legal items we covered; of all that, you want to know if I love my son like a son?" I'm incredulous.

"Yeah," she says, looking me in the eye for the first time that afternoon. "I've never seen an adopted kid with his mother before. I'm just curious. Do you love him?"

That's why the Bible talks so much about love. It is powerful and can break through tremendous strongholds and absolutely fascinates a world that has never seen it.

"Yes" I laugh, "That one is easy. I love him. I love him like crazy. I couldn't love him more if I wanted to."

Six months later, she holds my hand while she goes into labor and delivers a little girl, whom we together place into the arms of adoptive parents.

Now that little girl — who survived her mother's attempt to abort her with a broken Coke bottle — has a story of her own. Her life and testimony will go on to encourage her future generations, her parents, and everyone who knows her and her story.

Once again I learn that God has the right to use what he has built to draw others towards himself.

Evan has heard his story countless times over the last ten years. I never tire of recounting it to him because ultimately it lifts my spirit every time. I believe more, trust more, and have more confidence in the Author of our story. I trust him more as a Rebuilder, Restorer, and Repairer of all things because I have seen his handiwork. And I get to kiss him goodnight.

SEVENTEEN

Mamá Martha

As you learn more and more how God works, you will learn how to do your work. We pray that you'll have the strength to stick it out over the long haul — not the grim strength of gritting your teeth but the glory strength that God gives. It is a strength that endures the unendurable and spills over into joy, thanking the Father who makes us strong enough to take part in everything bright and beautiful that he has for us.

Paul (Colossians 1:9 – 12 MSG)

Squinting into the sunlight, I see shacks in every direction — homemade out of plastic, wood, scrap metal, broken block. Inside each one is a family. I'm visiting each family to see if they have a special "Easter burden" that we can pray for this morning.

Who am I kidding? "Easter burden"? Try "daily burden," I think as I see women washing clothes in a river and babies walking around without diapers.

The trick for me today will not be to lead them to the cross, but to go back and show them the empty tomb. Even here, there is hope.

Oh dear Lord, I pray, *please show up today.*

"Mom, we haven't been down that road yet." Emma points down a little pathway leading toward the riverbank. It's only April and already the sun is relentless.

Having already been to a dozen homes and hearing about more needs than I can ever conceive of helping, I am starting to wear down.

An Easter burden lifted

"Okay, one more," I say, "then we head for some shade." I playfully tousle the hair of my eight-year-old.

Lord, give me some of that "glory strength," I silently pray.

It has been a time of feeling like we have more work to do than we can possibly accomplish, more children to reach out to than we have helpers, more funding needs than anyone can meet. Recently I've been reading everything I can on time management ("Jesus *walked* from town to town," "he went to bed without healing everyone," "touch all things on your desk only once," "tithe your time in the morning and watch it multiply," and so on), and I still find it a struggle to balance my day-to-day activities. I'm a slave to my planner; I choose the urgent over the valuable more times than I want to admit; and I am sick of hearing myself talk about balance. I wonder do I have too much stuff?

I walk down to the shacks that line the river. "*Buenos días,*" I cheerfully greet the little girl standing in the dirt. "Are your parents home?"

"Not now," she answers shyly, her eyes full of fear.

Not wanting to scare her, I try a different approach. "We're here to pray with anyone who wants to talk to God about the worries they may have. Do you have something you want to pray about?"

She turns on her heel and walks back to her door, which has only a sheet covering the entryway. *Was that an invitation?* I wonder. Just as I am leaning over to Emma to tell her we will pray right here in front of the little house, the girl comes back out.

"*Sí*, I have something I am worried about," she says. "Will God do anything about it after we pray?"

"He is not a magician, so we can't ask him for a trick, but we can share with him how we are feeling and what we're afraid of, and he'll comfort us as we begin a relationship with him. Would you like that?" I follow her as she leads us into her one-room home. By the time I finish my sentence, we are in the doorway.

The house is about ten feet by ten feet. Inside are five small children, the youngest in diapers. There is no food, and the lack of cleanliness makes me wonder how long my new young friend has been left in charge.

"What is it you want us to pray for?" I ask.

"We're hungry." She doesn't ask for her parents to return or a bike or a better house. She just wants food for herself and her siblings. We bow in prayer: "Lord, would you bring nourishment to these children and make them hungry for you. Amen."

And then I decide that I can "fix" the problem.

After promising that we'll return in just a little while, Emma and I walk to a nearby food stand, where I buy several days' worth of groceries. I hope this will be the answer to their prayers.

We return and spend some time cleaning up and arranging the food on their makeshift table.

"I'm going to let the pastor know about your needs. I'll keep praying for you and for your mother's safe return. God bless you." I hug her. "And happy Easter." I feel good inside and so does Emma. We are leaving them in a better situation than we found them.

As we walk away, I put Emma up on my shoulders. But when we're about a block from their house, Emma yells down to me, "Mom, turn around, go back! Quick! There are people all around those kids' house!"

Sure enough, I hadn't even noticed that we were being watched as we walked back to their home earlier, our arms full of groceries and my heart full of good intentions. All the neighbors knew those kids were alone, and now they've come to steal the food. By the time we reach the door of the shack, a number of very unfriendly people are milling around.

Crying, the oldest girl looks at me accusingly and says, "Is this how God answers prayers?"

Flustered by her question, by the people standing around, and by my daughter whose eyes echo the same doubt, I panic. Oh God, what's going on? Please intervene!

God certainly doesn't delight in our fear, but I do think he sometimes politely waits to act until we've tried our own solution and failed. Then what he loves is the dependence with which we cry out to him. What a mess I had made. To be honest, I wanted to be able to imagine those children filling their bellies so I would not feel so guilty about filling mine. *Lord, forgive me!*

But as I cry out in his name, my heart is flooded with peace. I know in that moment that he's staking his claim over this shack. It feels like a wind blowing, but there's no movement in the trees. Where the Accuser had been just moments ago, stirring up fear and trouble, the army of angels is beginning to swoop in. There was an obvious change in the atmosphere. One of the Enemy's favorite tricks is to fill the air with fear and tension, but now, slowly, people begin to walk away, and peace settles over the shack.

The children and I walk over to a woman in the community who is respected and knows everyone and everything.

"These kids' mamá disappears for days at a time to work," she says as she peers at them. Then she scolds them, "Why didn't you come out sooner and ask for help?"

Without waiting for an answer, she looks at me, and I find myself standing up taller. "I will keep an eye on them until their mamá comes home" she says. I nod in appreciation.

The oldest girl, falling into a heap, begins to cry softly. At that point, Emma and I hug them goodbye and move away, and I let this woman begin to minister to her with an understanding of that life I do not share.

The girl cried out for food an hour before, and God provided so much more that afternoon. I don't know where they are now. As in most shack communities, families tend to be transient, but I have faith that the angels I felt swoop in that day haven't left them. I also pray that the oldest girl has the "strength to stick it out over the long haul — not with the grim strength of gritting [her] teeth, but with the glory strength that God gives." It will give her the strength to endure the unendurable … until one day it "spills over into joy."

That day I started out gritting my teeth. I looked around at needs that I had already determined were too weighty for me to handle in one morning. House by house, I gathered their Easter burdens in my own basket, until I lost sight of why I was there. Teeth-gritting and burden-carrying can do that to you. They cloud your vision. And what a glorious vision he wants to offer us on Easter morning and every other morning on which we can't see past our planners.

I can feel sick for the hundreds of thousands of little girls who bear burdens they weren't meant to. I want to blame someone. Is it the government's fault? Society's? Their mothers'? The absentee fathers'? I want to blame the church. I'd like to say it's because of the economy or the war. But it's all of those reasons and none of those. Can we ever make sense of it? Is it worth it to try?

Today, I cannot be in Indonesia or the Sudan or Guatemala. I may never make it to the Philippines or back to Eastern Europe. Today I am in Monterrey, Mexico. And while I will not shut my eyes to the needs of those other regions, I am reconciled to the fact that those burdens are someone else's to carry. I am called to Monterrey.

If it really is God's idea to pursue orphans, and really his timing and his plan, then it makes all the sense in the world that I would use *his* strength to participate in this movement. It means that all my time management issues probably suggest I'm taking responsibility for more than I've been asked to.

But I'm guessing the answer to my struggle is found somewhere between "letting go" and "praying for glory strength." And if, after prayer, there is no response, no surge, no remarkable offers to help, then is it possible I am asking for strength to set up my own kingdom and not God's?

People are drawn to Martha, not for what's on the surface, but for what lies underneath. God has built within her layer upon layer of a faith that seems relentless. I want to peel back some of those layers, so I ask her how it all started for her. How did she gain her ability to choose character over what feels comfortable? How did she learn such reckless faith? At first she waves her hand in front of her face, as if to swat away so many flies. But I can be a bit relentless myself, so I pester her (nicely) until she finally settles down to tell me her story.

"Well, it was sometime after my husband died," she begins, "that I found myself alone late in life," she begins, "and I became drawn to people who needed mercy. I simply wanted to focus on others. So I started in the jails and the slums." I sit back in my chair, knowing she will both draw this out and come right to the point.

"I used to stand up in church and tell everyone that on the weekend I was going to this jail or that drug house, and I'd practically beg people to come with me. But they wouldn't. So for four or five years, I went mostly alone to minister to the people."

Todd, Mamá Martha, and staff friend Gabriel Velasco

"Were you ever in danger? Were you afraid?" I lean forward, curious.

"I was more afraid of what would happen to me if I stayed home than if I went!" she laughs.

"As God would have it, he left me feeling dissatisfied; he gave me a sense that there was something else to come. Eventually God directed me to what he wanted me to do: minister to orphans."

I say, "Since statistically 90 percent of orphans end up in the black market or prostitution, in essence, God was calling you to those same people — but before they got themselves in those messes."

"Yes, that's true, though I always thought of it as taking care of the children of the prostitutes and prisoners."

"Did you have people telling you that you should just live out the rest of your retirement in peace? That you deserved it? Earned it?" I ask.

"Oh, yes, most people tried to stop me, though I don't know why. I feel most alive when I am ministering. I think some people just found it too tiring to worry about me," she said.

She faced many challenges at the beginning. Land, staff, funds — all were burdens that she lifted daily to the Lord. "If this is what you want ...," her prayers would always begin.

Slowly, the pieces started falling into place. Land was donated, staff appeared, funding trickled in — just enough to open her doors. She found herself dipping into her own savings many months to balance the books. "But it's all the Lord's money anyway," she insists.

Wouldn't it be great if after we make a difficult choice, after we start down a path of God's leading, our affirmation would come in the form of easy days and easy ways? As I listen to Martha talk about her orphanage's beginnings, I wonder whether *struggle* is the confirmation that we're on the right road and whether blue skies are actually a warning sign. I suggest this to Martha.

She replies, "We *are* in work opposed by our Enemy." Then she smiles as she adds, "It's all worth it, though, when I walk out of the office and hear shouts of 'Mamá Martha.'"

She has been mamá to over a hundred children in the ten years since her home opened its doors. Patiently and quietly she has lifted their eyes from their circumstances up to a God who she believes has a purpose for every life.

She tells another story: "A couple of years ago, I woke up at 3:00 a.m. feeling a burden for some unpaid bills. I just told the Lord, 'I am the servant; you are the King. You provide for your work, and I will gladly continue, but I cannot muster it up anymore.'

"The next morning, your husband, Todd, came to tell me of a sponsor who agreed to cover the orphanage's expenses for at least a year. Ever since that day, I wake up every morning at 3:00 a.m. to read my Bible and remember what the Lord did that night."

That's Martha — character over comfort.

Now in her seventies, she still works full time but admits to occasional fatigue. "There'll be time to rest on the other side," she tells me when I voice concern. "But today, there's still work to do."

As I drive home that day, I think about the truth I learn from Martha. She doesn't view herself as God's teammate, as she reaches out to the children in her home. She sees herself as an extension of God's care. They aren't working in tandem. God is the Source and she is the outlet. And what he has to offer will never run out.

Life had offered her two choices. One looked more appealing — with less work, less pain, less stress, and less heartache. It would have been the socially acceptable thing to do and a relief to those around her if she had just quietly lived out her retirement in peace. But she chose a harder path, and although it's been tough, by her own testimony, she feels richer, fuller, more satisfied, more loved, more alive. Who wouldn't want that quality of life?

We are constantly advised to take care of ourselves (which is important) and to maintain balance (which has value); but it can be tempting to stop when the Spirit is still saying "Go!" Instead of listening to ourselves and knowing our own limitations, shouldn't we listen to the Spirit and heed his direction? Sometimes that might look like stillness when we want activity. Sometimes that means avoiding activities that produce stress and self-importance. Still, sometimes that means working when you're tired, listening when you have other plans, or giving up when you'd rather not. It means understanding that on your own, you cannot help or listen or serve or share or work or accomplish anything of value if it's not done with God's strength. His is the strength that endures the unendurable and spills over into joy.

Marlene and Marilin

I was in junior high school in 1986, when my twin girls were being born in a village outside of Monterrey, Mexico.

Their transition from the orphanage to my home came in the spring of 2001, when we had a *quinceañera* for them (a fifteenth birthday celebration for Latin girls). I'd spent lots of time over the last couple of years having them over at my home, so I was anticipating a fun time at the local roller-skating rink with their friends. When the night of the party came, however, it was a disaster for reasons I couldn't even understand at the time. Everything seemed to go as planned. But these girls felt a deep sadness because no parent was present at this important rite of passage. It was like a black cloud was hanging over the night.

Marlene and Marilin, with me in between, celebrating their twenty-first birthday with a "princess" party, saying goodbye to childhood.

That was April 22. In my heart I could feel stirrings that something was wrong. These girls had spent more time in our home than any of the other children we worked with — so much so we felt especially connected to them. In another month, I knew, they would graduate from junior high, which marks the end of mandatory education in Mexico, and they had no plans for the future. Where would they go? What work could they do? Would we ever see them again?

I was about to find out.

Todd and I are like fireworks. Our relationship never coasts. It stalls and then bursts ahead. I didn't even know what I was looking for in a man, but I knew I had found it once we started dating.

One of the first guys I ever went out with was nice enough. One night he asked me where I'd like to eat, so I chose a new restaurant in town, and we had a great meal. We enjoyed that same restaurant for the following seven Saturdays — in a row.

In his defense, he was just trying to please me. But from my perspective, I didn't find it engaging. If I'd married him, maybe I'd still be eating at that same restaurant. Instead, I was longing for adventure — spiritual adventure — the kind where you understand you have one shot at life and you want to live it fully. That man was godly in many ways, strong and stable, undoubtedly someone's ideal of the perfect man.

But not mine.

That same year I met Todd. It was during that time that I invented an arbitrary measuring stick to decide whether I wanted to go out with a date again or not. I decided I would judge my dates according to how decisive they were when they ordered food. If a date took too long deliberating over his order, I deemed him indecisive and preoccupied with unimportant details, and I wouldn't go out with him again.

When the waiter came up to Todd, however, he ordered not only his meal but mine as well — without even looking at the menu! How much more decisive can you get? Could this be the guide I needed for my lifelong journey? While some girls might have balked at someone taking control of what

Here I am with Todd

they were going to eat, I was drawn to his confidence, at the risk he took not knowing how I'd react.

Our personalities couldn't be more different, but God brought us together for a purpose. Simply put, we are better together than we are individually. Todd completes me and balances out every place where I fall short. When I sprint, he marathons. When he reacts, I respond. When I start, he finishes. When he thinks, I feel. When we decide to bring out the best in each other, it's breathtaking. But when we use our energy and emotions to bring the other down, it's ridiculous how fast the fire can burn the whole house down.

In an age when we are told to be healthy individuals, seeking self-fulfillment and avoiding dependency, the biblical model still holds true: the more we serve each other and become one flesh, the stronger, not weaker, we become. By marrying Todd, I've actually become more of who I was created to be, not less.

One evening, he says, "Beth, what would you think if I said that I have been wondering what it would be like to bring the twins here permanently?"

He has just returned from a Father's Day event at their school, filling in as their father, and I think maybe he's had a few too many chili peppers.

"Like ... as in, all the time? Adoption? Stay here with us?" I'm feeling resistant, looking around at all the roles I'm trying to balance and wondering if there's room for one more.

He continues, "I think the Lord is asking us to make a commitment to the girls, and I want you to start praying about it."

So I pray, although a bit reluctantly at first. The *idea* of having them in our home, I think, is more exciting than the *reality*. But whoever said "prayer is more for us than for God" was on to something. After a while, I feel my heart moving in the same direction. I try to picture what it would look like to have them in our house, at our table, in our family pictures. I'm feeling excited and then terrified — and then both at the same time. There are lots of things I don't know about raising teenagers, but having just been one ten years earlier, I think, it couldn't have changed that much, could it?

One afternoon, about a month later, as I'm dashing in the door, I hear Todd's voice on the speaker phone: "Beth, pick up the phone!"

Balancing our toddler, Josh, on one hip and keeping an eye on Emma and Evan, I answer the phone. "What's wrong?"

"Someone's here to pick up the girls — and I don't think they have their best interests in mind. I'm going to try to intervene, but get over here quick! Pray we aren't too late!" And with that, he hangs up.

I drive to the children's home, knowing in my heart the decision has already been made. If God is truly leading us, then he knows the answers to all my remaining questions. It is a moment of reckless faith like none other I'd ever experienced to date. Sometimes, in those kinds of reckless-faith moments, the jump comes a split second before you're really sure there's water below. This is not one of those moments. This is a jump so high, I think, I may not know for years whether there is water below me.

But then it comes over me, even while I'm panicking — that inexplicable, doesn't-make-sense-at-the-time, peace-that-passes-understanding feeling. Todd and I step up to the edge, hold hands, and jump, by offering the girls a permanent home that same afternoon.

They came home with us that weekend in 2001, and they haven't left since. That fall, they attended high school, and now, as I write this, they are college graduates.

Taking in two teenage girls with their background and our lack of experience could have been a disaster, but God promises to be the father to the fatherless. He has in every way coparented with us. When we've needed wisdom, he has given it, and when we've needed patience or grace, he has always supplied it in abundance.

In those early days, when we struggled with communication and with the obstacles their past put in our way, I reminded myself that it was God's desire that we be a family and he brought us together. I clung to Colossians 1:17: "He is before all things, and in him all things hold together."

I wish I could say that following God's will in building our family led to many sweet days, that we sat around holding hands all the time. The truth is our God cared so much about their healing that he was interested in doing *whatever* it took to bring their hurt spots to the surface.

And we had a front-row seat.

In traditional parenting, you have years to teach your children to chew with their mouths shut or to write thank-you notes; you have windows of time when they think you're the greatest, and you use those years to mold and influence their interests, spiritual worldviews, and even which sports team to cheer for. We quickly realized we could not cover fifteen years of parenting in our first year together. The girls would have felt like projects and not people. I also didn't want their days to be filled with pointing out who they aren't, instead of who they are. So we majored in the majors and let them eat how they wanted and dress how they felt most comfortable. We focused almost exclusively on their hearts. Who were they sharing it with? How did they respond to hurts? When did they feel most alive? Could they trust all that with Jesus?

In turn, we asked those same questions of ourselves, and once again God's will was clearly multipurpose. He not only wanted to wake their sleepy spirits, but in the process he wanted to woo ours as well.

Did we have slammed doors and fights? Absolutely — about boys, dishes, curfews ... Did we cry at times? Yes — over misunderstandings, fear of the future, hurt feelings, unmet expectations.

During this time Todd and I thought we had the ultimate parenting tool: they couldn't speak our language. Our code names for them were "long hair" and "short hair" — as in, "Long hair wants to go over to her friend's house but didn't clean her room. What do you think?" — and all the while, they never knew they were being discussed.

Then one day we came home and found a note from them in Spanish, detailing for us where they'd gone that afternoon, and at the bottom, in perfect English, they wrote, "We'll be back for dinner; Love, long hair and short hair."

We laughed so hard that afternoon, and we wondered how long they had actually understood what we'd been saying.

A year after they came to live with us, we all sit down on the living room floor, with a Bible in front of us, to do a check-up on our lives together. I turn to a passage in Joel that illustrates God's promise to them and hope the timing is right to share it with the girls: "What the gnawing locust has left, the swarming locust has eaten. And what the swarming locust has left, the creeping locust has eaten. And what the creeping locust has left, the stripping locust has eaten" (Joel 1:4 NASB).

We ask if they can envision those crops being eaten by locusts. We talk about how metaphorical locusts have buzzed into their lives, eating layer after layer — those are the locusts of abuse and neglect, of lies and all the other activities that the Enemy uses to diminish God's glory.

I tell them, "The book of Joel goes on to say in chapter two, verse thirteen, 'Now return to the Lord your God, for He is gracious and compassionate, slow to anger and abounding in lovingkindness and relenting of evil.' That is the secret. I'm sure he will reveal to all of us the paths we need to take on our journey to your healing, but the guidebook, the Bible, is clear: the first step is to return to him."

We spend the rest of the evening talking about their dreams. What do they want to study? Where do they want to live? With whom? What kind of life can they imagine for themselves? We also talk about who in their lives have been locusts. What do locusts look like and how can we send them away when we hear them coming?

Todd prays, "*Señor*, be with our precious daughters whom you have created for a purpose. Help us to guide them down a path that offers more than we could ever ask or imagine. Amen."

I look at Todd as he prays, and I see a completely different person than the Todd of just a year ago. He is more thoughtful, more sensitive, less willing to tolerate locusts. A funny thing has happened as we have raised these girls: we've drawn closer together. In fact, being in over our heads has made us reach up to God, and like the sides of a triangle, as we move upward, we can't help but draw closer together. We now laugh about memories no one else finds funny or when one of the girls says something that nobody but us gets. We feel protective when someone is insensitive toward them, and most of all, we love hearing them call us "Mom" and "Dad."

A redeemed life, no less than the highest mountain, is a marker that points to the Creator. Who but God can rebuild us into something stronger, using even the weakest part of our past to strengthen us?

In raising Marilin and Marlene, we had no idea where or how to begin. We would wake up in the middle of the night and ask for guidance: What should we allow? What should we share? What things should we force them to do, and which should we let go?

Slowly, the buzzing of their locusts began to subside as the girls became better at hearing God whisper deep truths into their hearts, truths like:

You are valuable.

You are special.

You have a destiny.

You count.

You are gifted.

You were created for a purpose.

I have a plan for you.

You are my child.

These truths are like "locust repellent," and as the locusts disappear, we become more equipped to spot them whenever they approach once more.

One day, years after we had read those passages from Joel together, I opened the Bible to that same chapter. God has a promise for all of us in the second chapter, which I didn't read to the girls at the time, because I wasn't sure they would have believed it. I have shown it to them since, and I know it has taken root in the fertile soil of their hearts. Joel 2:25 – 26 (NASB) says, "Then I will make up to you for the years that the swarming locust has eaten, the creeping locust, the stripping locust and the gnawing locust.... You will have plenty to eat and be satisfied and praise the name of the Lord your God who has dealt wondrously with you."

He has made good on his promises — just as we knew he would. He is already making up for those years in the girls' lives that the locusts had eaten — in ways they will never forget. They have made peace with those years, and they have also gained a strength they will carry with them forever.

"Todd," I look over at him on Christmas Eve, "is this how you always imagined it?" Our children are strewn around the living room all around us, the little ones and the big ones all together eating more sweets than they should, watching Christmas movies, and waiting for midnight.

"No. No way. Not here. Not like this. Not this many—and not with you!" he teases.

"Yeah," I say, "I love it too."

NINETEEN

Meme

A person who makes the wildest claims, has the biggest ideas, and can stir up the largest crowd usually ends up being labeled a "visionary."

For me, a "visionary" is that person who has spent so much time with the Master they see circumstances completely from his perspective. For instance, when they're told, "It can't be done," they build arks, part seas, and believe in virgin births. And when they look into the eyes of an orphan, they see the child of a King. Now *that* is vision!

"There are two kinds of learners in the world; can anyone name them for me?" The professor drones on and on. It's my first day of class for the new semester, and as students, we are disappointed that he didn't just pass out the syllabus and send us home.

No one answers the question.

So the professor tries another tack: "If anyone can tell me what the two kinds of learners are, I will give them a passing grade without having to attend another class!"

Now he has my attention.

After we all painfully admit we have no idea, he begins his lecture with two questions: "How many of you would be willing to watch a movie without knowing how it's going to end?" (Some hands raise, not mine.) "And how many have no desire to volunteer for a committee or a group project until you have established the purpose and final outcome?" (More hands raise, mine the highest.)

"All right, then," he continues. "There are two kinds of learners: part-to-whole learners and whole-to-part. The faster you understand yourself, the way you teach, and the ways your students learn, the better off you'll be.

"A part-to-whole learner wants to solve the math problem meticulously, confidently knowing they've left nothing undone. The whole-to-part learner, by contrast, wonders, 'When will I ever use this in real life?' A part-to-whole learner never reads the last page of a book; he wants to ride the wave of suspense until the end. A whole-to-part learner won't read a book without a strong recommendation from someone and even still sometimes sneaks a look at the last page."

I am a whole-to-part learner. I want to know the point of something before I commit to it. I want to know where things are headed before I jump on board.

So imagine my learning curve when I confronted this fact: having "vision" means listening to the Lord and taking the next step in faith. Many people teach that vision is being able to see farther ahead than the other guy, but I've found it's just the opposite: vision is *not* knowing the end game ahead of time.

Having vision means experiencing growth. In ten years I'll pick up this book, shake my head, and think, "If only I knew then what I know now." Having vision, listening to God, and stepping out in faith all mean that my life experiences are building within me principles that I need for God's next call. They are the path I'm being led along — a path whose end I cannot see.

For instance, when we moved to Mexico, we prayed simply, "Lord, we ask that fifty people will come visit us this year to serve alongside us in this ministry." That seemed an unattainable figure. By the end of that first year, however, over 350 people had visited us. Our vision was nothing compared to God's!

Too often people think of the pastor with the largest congregation as the true visionary, while another pastor, who has ministered to the same small group year after year, is seen as stuck. Of course, the opposite can just as easily be true. The faithful pastor of a small church might have the greatest vision for his flock, while the megachurch pastor might easily be a good speaker and little more. God's idea of vision isn't about numbers. The foster mom who believes in the value of the difficult child placed in her care might have more vision than the head of a large and thriving children's ministry.

So what is vision if it's not big plans and big ideas? As I said before, it's primarily seeing events and people from Christ's perspective.

And living with Meme has taught me a lot about seeing things from Christ's perspective.

Rejected at birth, Meme was passed on to a relative who treated her as a servant rather than a family member. She was also "loaned out" to neighbors for manual labor and was denied basic affection.

Meme and me

"Meme," her adoptive mother would say to her when she was about eight years old, "if you're good this week and do all the laundry, then maybe we can go to the park on Sunday."

Always the same promise. Meme sighs and scurries out to wash the rest of the clothes in the basin. I don't know why I should believe her this time, Meme thinks to herself, but I do.

When she was fourteen years old she was married off to a widower more than a decade her senior, and while other teens were worried about their pimples and phone calls, she was giving birth and trying to survive while her husband squandered their earnings.

One night there's a knock at my door.

"Beth, are you in there?" I hear a voice from outside.

"Meme!" I exclaim, opening the door. "It's been years. How you have been? What have you been doing?"

I first met Meme while she was working at one of the orphanages with her family. Her husband, the widower, had become a believer through an employer, and a short time later, Meme became a believer as well. Together, they and their children served for more than a decade in the Christian children's home close to our house. After they left a few years back, I lost track of them.

"I was wondering," she mutters humbly, not making eye contact, "could I come in and offer my cleaning services? I'll exchange you work for some food."

"Meme, you know I'd be happy just to give you some food, but if you really need work, we can figure something out."

One of the women in the rio

And so we renew our friendship that day, she and I — and it's a friendship that has changed both our lives. I have given Meme employment, and a half decade of discipleship, but what she has given me is far more impressive: her vision.

She voluntarily lives in a squatter village, staying there for more than twenty years, so she can share the gospel with those around her. "Voluntary poverty?" I have heard of such things, but I've never met someone who lived it out — until I met Meme.

Meme sees people for *who* they are, not *what* they are, and as clichéd as that sounds, it rarely happens. Through her example, I now see a daughter instead of a prostitute, an adult orphan rather than a wife beater, and a desperate mother instead of a drunk. She has taught us to look at the people we serve who live in the most desperate of circumstances in terms of their relationships rather than their labels. And then with a faith God built brick by brick with his own hands, I see Meme trust him for provision and healing where most would throw up their hands (or at least wring them) and walk away. As a result, he provides and heals, and those relationships slowly walk toward restoration.

There is an expression in Spanish when someone unexpected comes to dinner; you just "add more water to the beans." I've witnessed God himself multiply Meme's "beans" to cover the needs that pile up on her doorstep. Jesus owns the cattle on a thousand hills and entrusts us with our own herd to administer according to his will and direction. As we spend and share those cattle, we store up for ourselves treasures in heaven. Although to the world, Meme looks poor, she is one of the richest ladies I know.

Last week Meme and I are talking over a situation involving her adult daughter, Jannette. Jannette and her family serve in a children's home, meeting an immediate, short-term need the ministry has. It is proving to be a challenge and her daughter calls Meme for comfort and strength. The Meme I know, who is always talking about boundless energy provided by the Lord, struggles because she knows how much this assignment from God is costing her daughter. One night, concerned about the fatigue she hears in her daughter's voice, Meme decides to encourage Jannette to leave the ministry and wait until her children are older before returning.

That night, Meme hardly sleeps. She tosses and turns and feels restless.

Early the next morning, her phone rings, and her daughter's cell phone number is displayed on the screen. When Meme answers it and says, "*Bueno, bueno* [hello, hello]," into the phone, no one responds, but she can hear the children from her daughter's orphanage singing her favorite praise song. She waits, but still no one responds. Meme then realizes the phone must have bumped something in her daughter's pocket and auto-dialed Meme's number. Meme sits back and listens to more songs, and she can pick out her daughter's voice and that of her oldest granddaughter singing praises to the King, surrounded by a choir of orphans at 6:30 in the morning.

After a while Meme hangs up, feeling a new peace. "Oh, thank you, *Señor*," she prays that morning on her knees. "Thank you for the measure you took to comfort a mother's heart that didn't deserve to question you." She now understands that God wants her daughter to stay at the orphanage despite the challenges.

Meme and I sharing the Gospel in the rio.

Later that day, when mother and daughter connect again, Meme tells her about the early morning call, and she encourages Jannette to stick with this assignment until the Lord releases her.

"But *Mamá*," Jannette protests, "the phone was in my room, and the keypad was locked! I was downstairs during the service, there was no way you could have heard us! Are you sure?"

When Meme names the songs that were sung and the exact time, they both fall silent, in awe of a God who cares about their relationship and a mother's concern.

As Meme recounts her story, I joke with her that she's on God's speed dial. Who among us wouldn't like to receive a call from the Lord to answer a plea we make in the night?

Vision is believing there is someone on the other side of our ceiling when we look up at night. It's trusting that the call had a supernatural origin and not a "logical explanation." Vision is believing in the relationship we have with a Creator who wants to show us people and circumstances from his perspective. Those children weren't bratty, uncontrollable challenges. They were *his* children, singing *his* praise, and designed for *his* good purpose. That's vision.

It's too easy for those of us to work with the poor to forget to address their poverty. We work around them or on behalf of them, but often we still don't know how they live or how to help. We have a responsibility to be God's hands and feet in their lives, for God cares about their hungry bellies, hurting feet, bug infested beds, and runny noses.

When we reach out without expecting anything in return—just to be a signpost that says, "God knows you are alive, he knows you have this need, and he sent me here to encourage you today"—the hardest heart can become momentarily softened. We then have the opportunity to water some seeds that God has planted. If we march into orphanages and poverty stricken communities and ignore the needs we find there, we will attract a few curious observers but we'll make little impact.

Through the vision of someone like Meme, however, we are able to understand the daily struggles that those in poverty face, and so we build relationships. It's harder to measure, messier to maintain, and makes our days more complicated, but it's through relationships that vision is born and eventually spread. That vision comes from seeing through someone else's eyes; it's the kind of vision God was speaking about when he fed four thousand people.

> *Jesus called his disciples to him and said, "I have compassion for these people; they have already been with me three days and have nothing to eat. I do not want to send them away hungry, or they may collapse on the way."*
>
> *His disciples answered, "Where could we get enough bread in this remote place to feed such a crowd?"*
>
> *"How many loaves do you have?" Jesus asked.*
>
> *"Seven," they replied, "and a few small fish."*
>
> *He told the crowd to sit down on the ground. Then he took the seven loaves and the fish, and when he had given thanks, he broke them and gave them to the disciples, and they in turn to the people. They all ate and were satisfied. Afterwards the disciples picked up seven basketfuls of broken pieces that were left over. The number of those who ate was four thousand, beside women and children.*

Matthew 15:32 – 38

Compassion doesn't originate in our bleeding hearts or moral sweat, but in God's mercy.

Romans 9:16 MSG

Meme's example has taught me one of the most important lessons I've learned: ministry isn't just your "day job." Although I try to gain balance in my ministry these days, I find I'm tempted to categorize my life into "ministry time" and everything else. Sharing my life with Meme has taught me that all my moments can be ministry — eating, cooking, washing, watching children, anything I do beside someone else, for someone else, or with someone else. I'm trying to make ministry and breathing and walking in the Spirit all the same action.

When Meme showed up at my door years ago, offering to work in exchange for food, I had no idea that we'd one day minister alongside her, bringing the gospel and food and housing to people whose lives at that time I couldn't have imagined.

But God knew.

God has ordained all of our days ahead of time (Psalm 139). He looked at Meme when she was only a small abandoned girl — and he saw who she would be today. He saw her walking around her village with her Bible in one hand and her pesos in the other, sharing God's love and concern for those around her. That's vision!

Todd and I are always being asked how many cities we'd like to be doing ministry in ten years from now. I could strike a "visionary pose" and say, "I hope we'll be in ten cities, serving ten thousand orphans and with a staff of a thousand." People might then shake their heads and sigh, "Wow! What vision she has ..."

But that's crazy. I have no idea if God will multiply this ministry or raise up another to minister to orphans. I have no idea if he will call us to go miles deeper where we are or miles wider where we aren't. I do know that he rarely reveals the whole story, which we whole-to-parters find so unsatisfying. He's much more interested in the development of my dependence on him and my relationship with him than he is in impressing me with his plans.

I already know he has big plans. He has an incredible track record.

So how much longer will we live in Mexico? I don't know. When I give my usual pat answer, "Until we're called somewhere else," people smile because it sounds so spiritual. And after all, I *am* a missionary. The truth is there are days (like today), when things don't get wrapped up in a bow, when there are more disappointments than victories, and when I want to pack up and go "home."

But for now, this is my home. No place on earth is really supposed to be home anyway; we are to be uncomfortable and restless until we are called to our eternal home.

"Vision" is that tonight I will continue to listen to the Lord and to feel his passion for the orphaned child run through my heart. Vision is a peace that today I have done all he created me to do.

Vision believes that I will wake up tomorrow and be used by him again. It is seeing every person's God-given potential and birthright. Vision is waiting and watching and knowing that God will repay the years the locusts have eaten. Vision is crying out for solutions to problems that are bigger than I can solve and knowing he will answer.

Vision is investing myself in lives that will blossom long after I've left the scene.

Vision is hope and faith in a God I cannot see, but who I believe has ordained my days and is working out all things according to his good purpose and will.

So how is vision accomplished? Not by doing or seeing, which always gets so much credit. It's by *listening* to his voice and taking the next step.

My friend Juan sits down with me on the bench. "So, how often do you actually enjoy a committee meeting?"

"Not often, unless I'm running it, I guess," I laugh and ask what he means.

"Well, I just went to my weekly meeting with the woman who is planning the youth rally," he says, "but we're hitting some roadblocks. People aren't doing their assignments; there are delays in contracts; it's been frustrating."

"... and you enjoyed that?" I tease.

"There are a lot of great people on the committee, and the leader has a good plan, but we're all feeling uninspired, and she could tell."

I laugh and say, "Sounds like lots of meetings I've been to."

"But then she asked us what we think she's doing wrong. It was really quite brave. I told her, 'I don't feel like you've allowed us to share in the vision. It's so "all yours" that I feel like I'm doing *you* a favor, which is fine, but that'll only take me so far. If I'm allowed to own the vision with you, and see how we're working toward a plan God has put on our hearts, I will work until I am bone tired and my fingers are bleeding. I'm sorry, it's just that my heart to work for God has a greater capacity than my hope that you appreciate my efforts.'"

"Did everything get quiet after you said that?" I ask.

"For a minute, until she realized what I said had some truth, and we're all going to pray about the plans and meet again next week. Now I'm looking forward to a meeting I was previously dreading."

If the new vision is from God then everyone involved will know it. To let go of control is to give vision birth.

Communion is just a snack unless you purpose to remember the Holy Spirit while you're eating and drinking. Washing someone's feet is just bathing unless you invite supernatural humility into the act. Worship can easily be relegated to singing when you forget the One on whom to focus. Baptism is only a symbolic swim if in your heart you don't believe you are now identifying with Christ. Praying is just poetry — or pleading — unless you believe someone is listening.

Vision is just planning ahead unless you take direction from the Lord. And perhaps *that* is the most reckless act of faith yet. It requires a letting go of *our* vision, *our* plans, *our* idea of what's good, big, best. A reckless faith trusts when God leads us down an unknown or lesser desired path. It trusts that the relationships we want to let go of — because they're too hard or too complicated — are actually being used for his glory, for our sharpening, and for the others' good. It trusts that this change, though difficult, is right because God sees farther down the path than we do. Vision is the natural byproduct of reckless faith because it's a *choice* to see ourselves as being woven into a bigger tapestry than we can see today. The vision starts and ends with God. It's not something we can muster up ourselves or dream up in our offices or committees. It's putting God's voice on the highest volume in our heads — and then letting go and being led.

So what's next as God pours himself out on behalf of the 143.5 million orphans worldwide? How do we address economic issues, healthcare, adoption? Do we need more agencies? Churches? Missionaries? Materials? Awareness? Dollars?

Some plotlines in the next chapter of my life I'm sure of. For instance, more and more people will commit their lives to orphan care — since it's a problem that is growing and warrants an entire movement — and more miraculous provisions will appear, more lives will be redeemed, more God-sized dreams will be dreamed. There will also be more heartbreak, more needs than we can meet, more children abandoned, more failed classes, and more missed opportunities.

But I can promise you that in the next chapter, those of us who work in this ministry won't stop until God tells us to. We will continue to fight and pray (and continue to invite you to do so as well) for the marginalized and abandoned children. We will serve children — sweating for them, defending them, and standing beside them — in the name of Jesus.

Please join us as we stay up late talking, worrying, praying for and with the child who is "waking up." Cry and laugh with us at their antics and delight with us in their successes. They need discipline, with consistency and humility, while they test their boundaries. Will you commit with us to provide them a home and lead them out of the darkness and loneliness? Will you be used by God to vindicate them, and every once in a while watch one be literally rescued?

Today we stand together and commit to share not only the gospel but our lives as these children watch us fall down, sin, celebrate, laugh, risk ... But we will not leave them, not until they ask to be left alone — and even then we'll keep pursuing them. As God leads us, we will come to them, hear them, lift them up, and be their parents. We will never forget that they matter to God and were created for a purpose and have a unique destiny. We will extend mercy toward them and be the recipients of their grace. We will give them food and clothing and be their helpers (in chores, in deciding which outfit to wear, in finding the right medicine, in thinking through their future). We will incline our ears, we will lift them up in prayer, and we will maintain their cause — not just until we are tired or embarrassed or uncomfortable, not just until we don't feel like it anymore — but we will maintain their cause until God comes again to bring us home.

I think it's remarkably fitting that the Lord ends his sixty-six-chapter book of education for us with a vision. It has been a source of conflict in the church, but Revelation is just that, a revelation of a time when God's vision will come to pass. I'm looking forward to that day when I am out of work, for we who know God will be adopted into his kingdom. There will be no orphans — only wholeness and belonging. Until that day, we trust in God and in his mercy and extravagant love. May he continue to show up — and show off — for his children.

> *Then I saw a new heaven and a new earth, for the first heaven and the first earth had passed away, and there was no longer any sea. I saw the Holy City, the new Jerusalem, coming down out of heaven from God, prepared as a bride beautifully dressed for her husband. And I heard a loud voice from the throne saying, "Now the dwelling of God is with men, and he will live with them. They will be his people, and God himself will be with them and be their God. He will wipe every tear from their eyes. There will be no*

more death or mourning or crying or pain, for the old order of things has passed away."

He who was seated on the throne said, "I am making everything new!" Then he said, "Write this down, for these words are trustworthy and true."

He said to me: "It is done. I am the Alpha and the Omega, the Beginning and the End. To him who is thirsty I will give to drink without cost from the spring of the water of life. He who overcomes will inherit all this, and I will be his God and he will be my son."

Revelation 21:1 – 7

Acknowledgments

After reading the acknowledgments pages of nearly every book I've read in the past many years, I've come to understand just how big an army it takes to produce a book.

First, I want to thank my husband, Todd, for encouraging me to keep writing back when this book was no more than a glorified journal entry. Todd, you made time when there wasn't any, and you made sacrifices so I could keep expressing what we were experiencing together. I cannot imagine this journey with anyone else.

Thanks to Jim Brazel, who was the first one to really believe in this book. Jim, I trusted you, and you were an unswervingly kind advocate and my entryway into the publishing world. Your introduction led me to Andy Meisenheimer, whose every comment made this book better. Andy taught me about more than just writing. The whole Zondervan team, including Bob Hudson and Karwyn Bursma, treated this project in a manner that made me grateful at every turn I was on their team. Thank you for the energy and prayers you put into your work.

I also want to thank the Back2Back Ministries Board and staff, both in Mexico and Ohio, who lived these stories beside me and have many more of their own. I'm humbled to serve beside you daily, and I believe God still has much more in store for us. To the staff women, thank you for all the times you prayed with me; your friendship makes me a better woman. I love living life with you.

To my friends at the James Fund: you've encouraged and inspired me. I stand in anticipation of what God will do next.

Katie Housh, my writing assistant, who read this book more times than anyone should have to: thank you for your attention to detail.

Lara and Corrie, who early on heard me dream about writing and kept cheering: I am grateful to call you friends.

Brad and Ben, with whom I'm proud to share our family heritage: you watched the Trooper pull out of the driveway that day and believed.

To Meme, who carried a heavy load with the grace of an angel: thank you for how you serve my family.

Lastly, to my children: You didn't ask to live this life, but you embrace it with blossoming reckless faiths of your own. I am so proud of you. We never know who will rest under our tree for a night, or a season, but I always know you will open your hearts. I love you more than anything . . .

Our family!
Top: Joshua, Aidan, Emma
Middle: Marlene, Evan, Carolina, Lupita
Bottom: Olga, Beth, Todd, Meme, Marilin

Share Your Thoughts

With the Author: Your comments will be forwarded to the author when you send them to *zauthor@zondervan.com*.

With Zondervan: Submit your review of this book by writing to *zreview@zondervan.com*.

Free Online Resources at
www.zondervan.com/hello

 Zondervan AuthorTracker: Be notified whenever your favorite authors publish new books, go on tour, or post an update about what's happening in their lives.

 Daily Bible Verses and Devotions: Enrich your life with daily Bible verses or devotions that help you start every morning focused on God.

 Free Email Publications: Sign up for newsletters on fiction, Christian living, church ministry, parenting, and more.

 Zondervan Bible Search: Find and compare Bible passages in a variety of translations at www.zondervanbiblesearch.com.

 Other Benefits: Register yourself to receive online benefits like coupons and special offers, or to participate in research.